FIELDS OF PLAY

The Sporting Heritage of Wales

FIELDS OF PLAY

The Sporting Heritage of Wales

Daryl Leeworthy

COMISIWN BRENHINOL HENEBION CYMRU

ROYAL COMMISSION
ON THE ANCIENT AND HISTORICAL MONUMENTS OF WALES

ISBN 978-1-871184-45-7

British Library Cataloguing in Publication Data.
A catalogue record for this book is available from the British Library.

Comisiwn Brenhinol Henebion Cymru

Royal Commission on the Ancient and Historical Monuments of Wales

Crown Building, Plas Crug, Aberystwyth, Ceredigion, SY23 1NJ

Telephone: 01970 621200   *e-mail:* nmr.wales@rcahmw.gov.uk   Website: www.rcahmw.gov.uk

Half title caption: **From the open-air swimming baths and the adjacent cricket pitch to the rugby ground raised up on a former spoil tip, this photograph of Maesteg, taken by the RAF in 1948, captures the many varieties of Welsh sporting heritage.**

Title caption: **Good kick by Moulder! Sport thrived in the densely-populated colliery communities and large numbers of teams came into existence from the 1880s onwards. Photographs such as this one were printed onto postcards and kept as souvenirs of a good match and the camaraderie fostered by watching and taking part.**

Printed in Wales by Gomer Press, Llandysul, Ceredigion.

Contents

Foreword by Eddie Butler

My earliest memories of sport involve going down with my father on Saturday mornings to light up the boiler in the wooden cricket pavilion at the bottom of Station Road, Raglan. I can still smell the mix of creosote, socks, putty and Mother's Pride bread. The socks often emitted the strongest of the scents and we would have to open the windows, an art in itself, requiring a blow hard enough to shift the jamb in the swollen frame but not hard enough to break the pane. The aroma of putty was a reminder that the six-year-old did not always master the art.

My father sat on the village Playing Field Association for years and so I knew a bit about the long-term lease of the cricket field from Neighbour Crump, whose name could not be bettered and whose farmhouse lay on the other side of the railway line that is now the A449 trunk road. The Crump land on that far side is now Raglan Golf Club. The cricket club no longer exists, but sport still goes on at the bottom of Station Road.

Cricket outdoors in the summer; squash in the winter. My father for years was also chairman of the Sports and Social Club at British Nylon Spinners, which became ICI Fibres, in Pontypool, and on Sunday mornings he would take my brother and me to the squash courts there. And from those courts to the skittle alley under the main clubhouse.

When I was older, I moved from those wonderful facilities on the Mamhilad site on the outskirts of Pontypool to the park in the centre, a landscaped jewel that used to be the estate around Pontypool House, built for Major John Hanbury, the ironmaster of the town. The rugby on Pontypool Park was not always as beautiful as the surroundings, but it had its own scent, of sweat and success.

In all those years, going from Raglan to Pontypool, with a little bit of the old Arms Park in Cardiff thrown in as it was swapping the red roof of the old South Stand for the cantilevered heights of the new National Stadium, I never probed any deeper into my sporting settings. As a six-year-old I knew about Neighbour Crump's gift of land to the village, but I don't think I asked a question – 'Where did all this come from?' – for the best part of fifty years.

And then I found myself in Brynmawr, presenting a *Hidden Histories* programme for BBC Wales. We were on the welfare ground built by volunteers in the 1930s, as was explained to me by Daryl Leeworthy of the Royal Commission. He knew about Brynmawr because it was part of his research for a book he was writing. Where did all this come from? Daryl had the answers.

And not just about Brynmawr. Raglan Cricket Club had been founded in 1824, on a field behind the Beaufort Arms, one of the first in Wales; British Nylon Spinners in Pontypool was just one of so many large companies that played their part in the history of sport by building facilities for its workers. Daryl knew why the rugby ground at Pontypool Park is elliptical, not rectangular. The shapes, roots, visions, tensions, successes and failures of where we play our sport in Wales are all here in Daryl's book, *Fields of Play*.

'It's just a field, like any other,' are words often used by coaches and players to reduce the sense of trepidation before a game away from home. In truth, the opposition's back yard is often more than that, although the power of home advantage is hard to analyse. Perhaps the answer lies in this book, in the sense of historical connection. The motives of landowners in the Victorian age for allowing conversion of certain parcels of their land into landscaped public parks may seem different from what inspired a party of Swiss and German volunteers to travel to the Heads of the Valleys during the Depression and build a swimming pool, but one thing in industrial and rural Wales had led to another and would lead again in a connected chain to what we have now, sport on grand stages: the Millennium Stadium; test cricket in Sophia Gardens; Ryder Cup golf at the Celtic Manor in Newport.

At every level in this process of developing world-class facilities there is a story. Each parcel of land has its own history of acquisition, every pavilion or clubhouse has had its own struggle to be built and every club has faced its own fight for survival. It is why we cherish our fields of play and defend them furiously. Daryl tells us this. And if I asked him how much pressure a six-year-old really should have applied to the windows in Raglan Cricket Club,

Pontypool Park

where the socks gave off a bit, I'm sure he'd know the answer to the nearest pound per square inch. Here, in detail and in overview, is most elegantly presented evidence that where we play is very much part of what we are.

Eric Butler

Preface

The origins of this book lie in an imaginative collaboration between the Royal Commission on the Ancient and Historical Monuments of Wales and Swansea University. Funded by the Arts and Humanities Research Council (AHRC), it gave one lucky researcher the opportunity to immerse himself in one of the most interesting aspects of modern society — sport and sporting heritage — and gain, at the end of it, a PhD. My starting point in that research was a photograph: it shows my grandfather and his school rugby team on a pitch in the Llynfi valley that, as I discovered later on, had been laid out by the miners of his village just a few years before. I then turned my attention to where I had played as a child — on the recreation ground in Ynysybwl — and its history was much the same. As I spoke to others during breaks from winding on microfilms or reading minute books, I became convinced that this was a story worth telling. All the more so given that much of what they spoke about has now disappeared from the landscape.

Many sources of information were consulted during the course of writing this book and took me on a journey from the south Wales valleys to Aberystwyth, Edinburgh, Switzerland and back again. Much of the research was carried out at the Richard Burton Archives in Swansea University, at Pontypridd Public Library, at Merthyr Tydfil Public Library and in the local studies department of Cardiff Central Library. Public libraries, university archives, public record offices, and the National Library of Wales are the lifeblood of work of this kind and I wish to thank every member of staff I encountered, and those that I didn't, who work there, but especially Katrina and Tony in Cardiff, Elizabeth, Sue, Sian and Katrina in Swansea, Hywel, Rachel and Edwina in Pontypridd, Carolyn in Merthyr and Anna at the Ceredigion Archives. I am especially grateful to Philipp Rodriguez, the archivist at the International Voluntary Service Archives in La Chaux-de-Fonds, Switzerland, for granting me access to their remarkable files on the Brynmawr and Rhos schemes of 1931 and 1932 and I would like to express my thanks to the staff of the *Bibliothèque de la Ville* in La Chaux-de-Fonds for providing such a genial work environment during my time there.

Photographic illustration is vital to a book of this nature and I have been fortunate in receiving the kind assistance of Bridgend Library Service, Cardiff Library Service, Newport Library Service, Rhondda Cynon Taff Library Service, Carmarthenshire County Museum, the Judge's Lodging in Presteigne, National Museum Wales and Pontypridd Museum. Tim Pettigrew provided several fascinating images from his family archive. Details of these photographs can be found in the table at the back of the book.

The remarkable series of historic aerial photographs that adorn many of the pages are housed at the Royal Commission's archive in Aberystwyth. Many of them were taken by the Aerofilms Company which was the UK's first commercial aerial photography company and founded in 1919 (the earliest photograph in this book taken by Aerofilms dates from 1920). Most of the others were taken after the Second World War by 540 Squadron, the RAF's photo-reconnaissance unit. Founded in 1942, 540 Squadron flew numerous sorties over Wales charting the progress of reconstruction after 1945. Unrestricted by civilian flying regulations and without the commercial demands that Aerofilms operated with, the RAF oblique and vertical photographs are an invaluable resource.

For permission to quote generously from the work of Gwyn Thomas, I am grateful to Jeffrey Robinson and the Gwyn Thomas Estate. Leslie Berry granted me permission to incorporate some of Ron Berry's writing and I am grateful to her and the Ron Berry Estate. I should also like to acknowledge and thank the Dylan Thomas Estate for their kind permission to use the passage from *Reminiscences of Childhood* at the start of chapter 1.

Many friends, family and colleagues (too many to list here) have given help and I am grateful to them all. Peter Wakelin encouraged me to write this book in the first place and has patiently guided it to fruition. Richard Suggett provided invaluable insight into the process of writing and publishing. Martin Johnes and Chris Williams supervised the thesis on which parts of the book are based and provided comments on various versions of the text.

Massed crowds at Ynysangharad Park awaiting the start of the international tour match between Glamorgan and South Africa, 18 May 1929. This was the first such match to take place in Pontypridd and came just three years after the ground began hosting first-class county cricket. The popularity of sport across ages and genders is apparent. South Africa won the match by 170 runs.

Eurwyn Wiliam, Scott Lloyd, David Toms and Vicky Davis read the entire text and made valuable suggestions to improve it. Medwyn Parry and Deanna Groom introduced me to and then guided me through the wonders of post-war RAF aerial reconnaissance. Helen Rowe provided hours of help with the Aerofilms archive and Penny Icke, Cheryl Griffiths and Frances Foster helped me navigate the treasure trove of the National Monuments Record.

Finally, thanks are due to those who transformed a typescript of text and a selection of images into the book before you. Fleur James breathed new life into the photographs and revealed many of the photographer's little quirks – such as drawn-in eyes and mouths – that had gone unnoticed for decades. John Johnston guided me through the finesse of giving a book an identity of its own and, with skilful flair, Owain Hammonds crafted the design. And, to Eddie Butler, who wrote a foreword that speaks to and captures the sense of where we play, which matters a great deal.

INTRODUCTION:
Up the Rec

When the Valleys from Blaenrhondda and Maerdy were heavily wooded, it used to be the practice for squirrels to take a daily hop down to Pontypridd. Some would start from Maerdy in the Rhondda Fach; their opponents from Blaenrhondda; and they would meet at Porth from whence they ran their races. This is the origin of sport in Rhondda....

H.W.J. Edwards, *The Good Patch* (1938)

Modern Wales might well be described as a land of goal posts and playing fields. It was not always this way (though the story does not exactly begin with squirrel races). From Victorian philanthropists to twentieth-century trades unionists and twenty-first century club members, people have shaped the urban and rural landscape for the purposes of sport and recreation. Much of what exists today reflects their varied interests. National arenas such as the Millennium Stadium in Cardiff, the Celtic Manor in Newport, and the Liberty Stadium in Swansea are evidence of the high profile of contemporary sport but, across the nation, villages and towns cherish more commonplace parks, playing fields, recreation grounds and swimming pools.

The everyday sporting landscape does not surrender its history easily but behind each playground lies a story of struggle, jubilation, and sometimes sadness. The making of the historic sporting environment is therefore a story not just of the hallowed turf upon which Wales defeated England many years ago but also, and more importantly, the people who made it.

Fields of Play is intended as a guide to the broad historical themes that have shaped spaces taken for granted by modern society. The historic environment constantly changes and its sporting facets are no different: each generation makes and remakes it according to its own needs and wants. The chapters that follow revisit public parks that lay at the heart of Victorian and Edwardian provision for recreation, the swimming baths and miners' welfare grounds of the 1920s and 1930s, national stadiums and the national parks that have turned the landscape of Wales into territory for sport, leisure, and pleasure.

The growth of the state from the middle of the nineteenth century, at first to deal with public health and eventually to encompass whole swathes of an individual's life, is perhaps the great story of political and social change in modern Britain. Today, the first park, swimming pool or playing field that most people use is owned and managed by their local council. The influence of local government is therefore pervasive, but it was not always this way. Indeed, for much of the nineteenth century commercial facilities dominated. The seemingly unstoppable expansion of organised sporting activity — whether rugby, football, or cricket — placed greater and greater demands on leisure space and a number of clubs struck out for permanent bases of their own. Many of these are famous grounds in their own right – Cardiff Arms Park, St Helen's, Stradey Park, or the Racecourse in Wrexham.

Yet the story of ordinary spaces, in ordinary communities, deserves to be told in order to complement the many histories of those fields of play. Elements of this tale can be found in novels and poems written by Welsh writers. Thousands of visitors, for example, travel to Swansea's Cwmdonkin Park in search of Dylan Thomas's 'world within the world of the sea town'. Such fragments reveal the importance of recreational spaces to the people of the past, and some even describe how they came into being. In his classic 1939 autobiography, *These Poor Hands*, Bert Lewis Coombes tells of a group of men from his mining village who, bored one afternoon during the National Strike of 1921, took up their downed tools and set about laying out a cricket pitch on a piece of waste ground. Mirroring the voluntarism common in the south Wales coalfield in this period, the group appointed a groundsman on the basis of his visit to

Taken at the Ynys Fields in Aberdare by local photographer Hans Hoyer, this photograph illustrates what many consider to be a typical Valleys' scene and one that neatly encapsulates what sport in Wales is all about: rugby on the rec.

MAESTEG WELFARE PARK WORKMEN
- APRIL 1931

Unemployed yet dedicated volunteers such as these men from **Maesteg** helped to build many of the parks and recreation grounds used in Wales today. With little prospect of a job, they set about transforming their communities and giving a better future to their children.

the M.C.C. and, having convinced others in the community to help with jerseys, bats, and a changing room, the cricket club was born.[1]

The alternative to voluntary effort was the local authority — the urban districts, rural districts, municipal boroughs, and county boroughs. Published in 1936 and capturing something of the spirit of the age, Gwyn Jones' *Times Like These* focuses on the great strike of 1926.[2] The young characters, having fallen on hard times during the dispute, are offered short stints working on public projects. The local authority of the novel (as in real life) offers jobs building a park for the community and so a sense of the value of work and the identity it helps to provide is restored along with something of its once-green landscape.

For the reconstruction planners charged with rebuilding in the aftermath of the Second World War and the Depression, the restoration of the landscape was a motivating factor.[3] The national parks of Snowdonia (1951), the Brecon Beacons (1957), and the Pembrokeshire Coast (1952), and areas of outstanding natural beauty such as the Gower peninsula (1956), were an expression of the desire to protect the landscape from the wrongs of the past as much as a mechanism for the promotion of tourism to economically stagnating rural counties.

This book's emphasis on how ordinary people transformed the landscape for sporting purposes is not to suggest that the orthodox history that sees public parks as spaces 'gifted' to the

...sea Riverside Albions A.F.C. 1926-27

Finding land on which to play sport in industrial areas was difficult and for many teams the home ground was a levelled-off patch of a nearby coal tip. Despite this, players took great pride in representing their communities and wearing the local colours.

people of towns and cities is wrong, simply that philanthropy is only a relatively small part of the broader picture.[4] It is indeed true that men such as George Grant Francis and William Thomas of Lân were at the forefront of demands for parks in Swansea, but what were the connections between the debate they held in the council chamber of Swansea Town Hall and working-class forms of recreation?[5] To restore the historical agency of working people to the story of the making of sporting space is, therefore, one of the primary aims of *Fields of Play*.

The importance of public recreation facilities to the history and ongoing cultural life of the working class has, of course, long been recognised even where the contribution of that class to their construction and maintenance has not. In a passage from his 1957 book, *The Uses of Literacy*, Richard Hoggart describes the atmosphere in a local swimming baths:

Go to them at four o'clock during the schools' term or on Saturdays. They are smelly with cleaning chemicals, chillingly angular, and slippery-scummy at the edges. But they ring shatteringly with the voices of working-class children throwing themselves and their friends in repeatedly, fighting in bunches in the water and blue with cold because they almost all stay in much too long.[6]

This reveals both the popularity of the collective experience of public recreation amongst working-class people (particularly children) and the social value of the amenity. It is easy to overlook that these were landscapes and buildings shaped by the people who paid for them, used them and were employed to work at them.[7] Whilst a park is, broadly speaking, an expression of the values of its designer, it is fundamental not to lose sight of the social forces that continually refashioned their meaning. Roy Rosenzweig, an American historian, has written that 'to think of public parks solely as works of art is to rob them of their complexity and to misunderstand their history'.[8] In writing about public recreation in Massachusetts, Rosenzweig put forward the case for leisure amenities as places that were fashioned by working-class people who built, transformed and infused public spaces with their own meanings and purposes and thus challenged the assumptions of philanthropists.[9]

Through the history of recreation, it is possible to see increasing freedom in society. Parks, in particular, gradually became more permissive and open to a variety of different recreational activities as workers exercised their political voice. Political representatives of organised labour found their way onto parks' committees and set about influencing not just the principle of providing a park or a swimming pool, but its location within working-class districts of towns and cities rather than professedly for all, but situated within middle-class areas. The struggle to loosen the restrictions on what was considered appropriate within the parks took longer to win, but the welfare grounds of the 1920s and 1930s aimed at being grand outdoor leisure centres in which mothers could rest with their toddlers on the park benches, young women could play tennis, and miners could play quoits, bowls, rugby, or soccer.

The chapters that follow examine the major forms of leisure amenities from the public park and swimming pool to sports stadiums and national parks. The opening of Cardiff's Sophia Gardens in 1858 marked the beginnings of a formal sporting environment and, at the same time, the passing of aristocratic dominance in the provision of public facilities. The period of greatest activity fell between 1880 and 1940 with the rise of local government and a widespread voluntary movement. Thereafter, two periods of growth can be discerned: from the late 1960s into the 1970s when much of the sporting infrastructure was renewed and more modern, multi-purpose leisure centres were built; and from 1997 as first New Labour and then the National Assembly invested on a similar scale. Both of these recent periods of renewal and growth occurred in response to national concerns. In 1960, the Wolfenden Report on Sport and the Community highlighted the broad inadequacy of Britain's sporting environment and the pressing need for refurbishment. It was quickly followed by a special report produced by the Central Committee on Physical Recreation on sporting facilities in Wales, which demonstrated the severe barriers there. The 1964 general election saw manifesto commitments from both Labour and the Conservatives on the provision of facilities for sport and Labour's additional promise to set up a Sports Council. Winning that election by a whisker, Harold Wilson's government founded the Sports Council for Great Britain the following year. The Welsh Sports Council was given its royal charter in 1972. Investment flowed from both.

The most recent expansion has followed concern about public health and the obesity epidemic. Concerns have focused on the more sedentary society promoted by indoor entertainments from satellite television to video games. Neglect of public facilities and the closure of numerous swimming pools over the course of the 1980s and early 1990s also necessitated significant investment. Between 1997 and the 2001 general election, financial support for new playing fields and sporting facilities reached almost £1 billion across the United Kingdom and investment continued to be made over the next decade as major sporting events such as the Commonwealth Games and the 2012 Olympic Games focused attention on the need for grassroots facilities.

Massive government spending in the late twentieth century is in complete contrast with the manner in which the sporting environment was constructed in pre-industrial times. Although this book does not dwell on early forms of sporting heritage, it is important to provide some context for what happened later. Perhaps the earliest form of arena for physical recreation and spectacle that survives in modern Britain is the Roman amphitheatres, of which there are four surviving examples in Wales: at Tomen-y-Mur in Snowdonia, Carmarthen, Caerwent in

---

Ancient games had a rather different quality from modern sports but required an arena nevertheless. That at Caerleon is the most impressive of those that have survived in Britain. Here it is shown opposite twentieth-century playing fields in a photograph taken by the Royal Commission's aerial reconnaissance unit.

Monmouthshire (although this has not been conclusively proven), and the largest and most impressive of all at Caerleon (on the outskirts of Newport).[10]

First excavated in the 1920s, the legionary amphitheatre at Caerleon serves as a reminder that sport is neither an exclusively modern phenomenon nor was pre-industrial sport limited to cock-fighting pits and Tudor tennis courts. Against the backdrop of up to 6,000 spectators, the gladiators who fought in the arena were the sports personalities of their day. Caerleon, of course, provided spectacle that was more akin to lower league football compared with the elite levels of gladiatorial contest found in the major Roman cities, but for soldiers stationed in

fortresses such as Caerleon or in more remote areas such as Snowdonia and for the townspeople of Carmarthen, the amphitheatre provided an important morale boost. Drawing on evidence from Pompeii of the rich material culture associated with sport, it is possible to imagine Roman fans in Britain scribbling graffiti on walls and staring at posters advertising contests sponsored by local elites.[11] With well-placed seats for rich patrons and seats 'in the gods' for poorer spectators, the Roman amphitheatre had segregation similar to that found in modern football stadiums. Without exaggerating the similarities between crowds enjoying bloodsports of the most lethal kind and those whose excitement might lead to jeering the referee,

Constructed c.1860, the handball court in Nelson is the surviving legacy of a very old game. Long thought to have been introduced by immigrant Irish workers, handball was in fact played across pre-industrial south Wales with communities such as Ynysybwl famous for its skilful players.

the football stadium and the amphitheatre exist as part of a continuum of sport across Welsh history.

In medieval and early modern Wales, the sporting calendar was focused on annual fairs. Bear-baiting, cock-fighting and foot racing all took place at fairgrounds with spectators standing around to watch. In Merthyr, the centuries-old Waun fair, which took place on the hills overlooking the town, was typically marked by horse racing and pugilist displays.[12] Similarly, in Ynysybwl, the fair provided the opportunity for local handball players to exhibit their skills.[13] The pandemonium of the games and the gathered crowds could be seen at similar fairs across the country. Bando, or 'bandy' as it was sometimes known, was a common sport throughout Glamorgan. Akin to shinty in Scotland, hurling in Ireland, or the more familiar hockey throughout England, it was often played on beaches, and teams from villages such as Aberavon, Baglan, Kenfig and Llantwit Major came to prominence as leading exponents of the game.[14]

Pre-industrial sports including bando and handball had designated places at which matches were played but the imprint of these sites on the environment was marginal. Handball players often played in churchyards or at public houses using the gable end and some chalk to mark the lines in place of purpose-built courts, which came later.[15] The practice continued for much of the nineteenth century even as the presence of sport was deemed a nuisance.[16]

With the emergence of parks, playing fields, dedicated recreation grounds and swimming baths, the landscape of sport was transformed. At the same time, miners' institutes and civic buildings came to encompass other aspects of leisure. It is from these more formal types of space that sporting heritage has developed.

In recent years, the issue of sporting heritage and what to do with it has risen to prominence as a result of the demolition of historic arenas such as Stradey Park, Ninian Park, and the Vetch. Less famous, local facilities including the vast majority of the open-air swimming baths that could once be found in public parks have also disappeared, either from neglect or having been replaced by multi-purpose leisure centres. Handfuls remain, including the lido in Ynysangharad Park in Pontypridd, which was once one of the largest open-air swimming baths in Britain and, despite its listed status, has suffered from decades of disuse.

Writing of the mining communities of the north-east of England, Alan Metcalfe has argued that for most miners 'sport provided the meaning of life […] more important by far, after survival needs have been met, than any other aspect of life'.[17] It is because of the popularity of sport that its impact on the landscape is ubiquitous. Yet for all that, the heritage of Welsh sport is remarkably ignored. Unlike in England where there is a National Football Museum, a National Rugby Museum and a National Cricket Museum, or in Scotland where there is the Scottish Football Museum at Hampden Park and the soon to be reopened Scottish Rugby Museum at Murrayfield, Wales has no national museums for any of its major sports. What remain to tell the story are history books and the marks made by sport in the landscape. It is hoped that *Fields of Play* will become a guide to the sporting heritage of Wales, a prompt for discussion on its future and, most importantly, a tribute to the people who made it.

CHAPTER I:

The Public Park

The park itself was a world within the world of the sea-town; quite near where I lived, so near that on summer evenings I could listen, in my bed, to the voices of other children playing ball on the sloping, paper-littered bank; the Park was full of terrors and treasures.

Dylan Thomas, *Reminiscences of Childhood* (1943)

The public park, with its grassy verges, bandstand and children's playground, is the quintessential, everyday form of open space for leisure. Parks are ubiquitous in the built landscape across Britain and provide for the general recreation of the entire population. Emerging in the middle of the Victorian era, they have since developed to meet demands for organised sport and more modern forms of activity from adventure playgrounds to skate parks. They have also seen the loss of facilities that were once markers of a certain kind of urban civility, such as the Victorian and Edwardian bandstands, which offered live music and entertainment to massed crowds and the many open-air swimming pools built during the economic turmoil of the 1920s and 1930s. The coming and going of such facilities reflected the prevailing focus of contemporary attitudes towards leisure and the purpose of parks.

Such facilities were in contrast to the very first public park in Wales, which opened in 1858. Sophia Gardens, which lie along the banks of the River Taff in central Cardiff, are traditionally considered to be the prototype. Laid out on the wishes of Lady Sophia, the widowed wife of the Second Marquess of Bute, the Gardens were instantly recognised as something new. 'In no town in the Principality', the *Cardiff and Merthyr Guardian* enthused, 'does such a pleasure ground exist'.[1] Designed by the Scots-Italian architect Alexander Roos, Sophia Gardens were intended to offer public walks through beautifully landscaped avenues lined with shrubberies leading to a central fountain and a bowling green.[2] At the northern edge of the gardens lay a boating lake whilst the southern entrance was flanked by a hunting lodge, designed by Roos in 1860–62, reminiscent of Castell Coch at Tongwynlais.

In the mid-nineteenth century, Cardiff was emerging as a major economic centre. With the completion of the Bute Docks and a new civic architecture in prospect, the town seemed a beacon of progress compared with what it had been. Government officials had found the town to be as riddled with Dickensian poverty and squalor as the very worst parts of Manchester or Edinburgh. The main thoroughfares of the town were inhabited by 'families bordering on pauperism'; yet it was recognised that Cardiff was 'certainly thriving and likely to improve'.[3] Sophia Gardens were part of this improvement. They offered a well-planted open space in which residents were permitted by the Bute Estate to enter for the purposes of 'rational recreation': walking through the pathways in one's Sunday best.

Sophia Gardens aimed at the transformation of the landscape of Cardiff and the attitudes and behaviour of its citizens, particularly those from poorer backgrounds. 'Judge my surprise', one correspondent of the *Cardiff and Merthyr Guardian* exclaimed in a letter to the editor, 'when on Sunday last I was refused admittance, with my two children, whilst a number of other persons had the gate opened to them and permission granted to roam at pleasure.'[4] This correspondent was not alone and the number of refusals of entry over the course of the summer of 1858 resulted in an attempt by the Trustees of the Bute Estate to restore their popularity. At the Bath and West Show, which was

Taken by Aerofilms in September 1959, this photograph illustrates the fusion of Victorian rational recreation — observe the tree-lined pathways and bandstand — and interwar sporting populism that marked Pontypridd's Ynysangharad Park as a new form of public amenity when it first opened in the summer of 1923.

The importance of Sophia Gardens and Bute Park as 'green lungs' in the centre of Cardiff is immediately apparent in this Aerofilms photograph of 1920. In the middle distance is the Arms Park, then a largely open ground, and in the background the bustling docklands and the mudflats. No barrage in those days!

held in the town that year, John Boyle, one of the Trustees, pointed out to the assembled visitors that the young Lord Bute intended that the Gardens be opened to the public and 'should from the present hour be permanently devoted to their service'.[5] Members of the Cardiff Local Board of Health, however, wrote to the Trustees to determine whether or not they intended to dedicate Sophia Gardens to the public in a formal way. Under pressure to be seen to be acting in the best interests of the town and its

people, the Trustees relented and general access was allowed from dawn until dusk. It was a victory for the council and finally established Sophia Gardens as a public park.[6]

The Emergence of Parks

The public park emerged in Britain primarily as a result of action taken by parliament and local councils in response to the increasingly dire situation in industrial towns in the north of

England. Although towns such as Merthyr Tydfil shared in the dirt and dust of the industrial revolution, Wales was largely neglected in this wave of development. In fact, the closest the parliamentary committee came to Wales was to hear testimony from a Bristol MP. Nevertheless, the parks in Manchester, Bristol and Leeds provided clear examples for local authorities. The first action by parliament was a select committee report on public walks published in 1833. It concluded that public walks would do much to improve the health, comfort and contentedness of working people and a series of bills were presented to the House of Commons in order to provide a legislative framework within which local boroughs would be able to act. Although none of

Laid out to mark Queen Victoria's Diamond Jubilee, Neath's Victoria Gardens (shown here as they were in 1929) are quintessentially nineteenth-century. Bandstand and tree-lined pathways offered rational recreation and footballs were kept far away. A people's park, then, for the leisure habits of only some of the people.

these passed into law, the impetus that they generated was clear and across northern England local authorities began to lay out open spaces that became affectionately known as 'people's parks'.

The people's parks provided well-planted, landscaped gardens and featured attractive walks. Providing a template for the classic Victorian and Edwardian parks such as Roath, Cwmdonkin, Victoria Gardens in Neath and Bellevue in Newport, they were not designed for mass physical recreation despite being intended to draw working people away from their traditional habits. In the words of the select committee:

> *Your Committee feel convinced that some Open Places reserved for the amusement (under due regulations to preserve order) of the humbler classes, would assist to wean them from low and debasing pleasures. Great complaint is made of drinking houses, dog fights, and boxing matches, yet, unless some opportunity for other recreation is afforded to workmen, they are driven to such pursuits.*[7]

In other words, the early public parks intentionally removed the capacity to participate in these 'debasing pleasures'. There was to be no space provided for football or cricket let alone dog fighting and boxing. Equally, the park was considered to be a place to visit dressed up: 'a man walking out with his family among his neighbours of different ranks', opined the members of the select committee, 'will naturally be desirous to be properly clothed, and that his wife and children should be also'.[8] Late into the nineteenth century, men and women travelled to the park in their Sunday best and parks committees sometimes found themselves liable for compensation claims when pairs of trousers were 'badly torn in an awkward place'.[9]

The earlier public parks in Wales were typically laid out in the major towns of Glamorgan where industry had begun to erase the green open space that had been present just a few years previously. In Swansea the construction of the South Dock in 1852 on the site of eighteenth-century pleasure grounds provided the impetus towards the eventual development of a network of urban public parks. Having revelled in its status as an 'intelligent town' in the late eighteenth- and early nineteenth-centuries, Swansea's leading citizens sought to reverse the impact of what they saw as the dangerous effects of rampant commercialism.[10]

It was, as George Grant Francis complained in the *Cambrian* in the 1860s, 'careless of questions of taste and too often destructive of the facilities of enjoyment and recreation which have existed

Erected in 1906 and designed by Ivor J. Thomas, this statute of William Thomas stands in Swansea's Victoria Park as a memorial to the Welsh Pioneer of Open Spaces. To the rear is the Patti Pavilion, once the winter gardens of opera star Adelina Patti, which was moved to the park in 1920.

for ages'.[11] Where once the Burrows had been the playground for a budding seaside spa town with its Royal Institution, theatres and learned societies, the arrival of the docks signalled the end of Swansea's Regency respectability: the magnificent vistas offered by Oystermouth Bay remained, but a place to wander amidst the flowers had gone.

Campaigning for public parks in Swansea began in earnest in the late 1860s and early 1870s when Francis' early efforts to promote the idea were developed by corporation member William Thomas.[12] Affectionately known as the 'Welsh Pioneer of Open Spaces', Thomas was at his political peak in the 1870s when the first public parks were developed in the town. Cwmdonkin Park was one of Thomas' notable successes. It was not, however, without controversy. Early efforts to lay out a park on land near Cwmdonkin reservoir had taken place in the early 1850s during George Grant Francis' time as a member of Swansea Corporation, but little came of them.[13] Instead, the surplus land was left vacant in order to provide spare capacity for Swansea's water supply and the open space became a place of leisure through common use. By the end of the 1860s, it was apparent that the demand for water supply was not forthcoming and the corporation planned to sell off some of the excess land whilst leaving only a small portion for a formal recreation ground.[14] The decision prompted angry responses. 'Why not lay this land out as a small recreation ground?' enquired an editorial in the Cambrian.[15] The following week, a correspondent suggested that:

Cwmdonkin has been for a long season the resort of thousands of our citizens, and the site, if well seated and pathed, and planted with trees and shrubberies, would be without exception one of the healthiest and finest resorts for pleasure-seekers, and those who need recreation, to be found in South Wales. Fancy the Bristol Corporation selling 'Brandon Hill'.[16]

This idea gained momentum and, with support in the council chamber from men such as William Thomas, Cwmdonkin Park was finally opened in 1874. Situated in one of Swansea's more fashionable districts 'where, in addition to the commercial magnates, live most of those artists, rhymesters, and other frivolous folk', Cwmdonkin was in keeping with people's parks elsewhere in Britain, which took the name but did little to provide

for the leisure of ordinary people.[17] Although, by the end of the nineteenth century, a bandstand was added to provide for public entertainment, in essence this was a pleasure ground designed for walking amidst beautiful surroundings. For William Thomas, who certainly recognised the flaw, the scheme contributed to the greater good. Nevertheless, he pressed fellow members of Swansea Corporation, insisting that they had misunderstood the problem: instead of simply providing open spaces wherever they could be obtained, it was important to locate them in areas of greatest need, where children had nothing 'other than the gutters to tumble about in'.[18] The Swansea Journal returned to the issue a few weeks later, arguing that the corporation ought to be responsible for:

Securing suitable plots of ground or open spaces available in the various thickly populated districts for the sons of toil to obtain a daily free breathing in pure air, and for the young children to run at all times from the 'streets and lands of the city' to enjoy their sports and amusements, instead of wallowing as they do in the gutters.[19]

This discussion prompted the donation of Knapllwyd Farm in 1874 by John Dillwyn Llewellyn. Located in a working-class district in the east of the town and opened in October 1878, Park Llewellyn (as it became known) helped to balance the provision of parks in Swansea. By the end of the 1880s, Victoria Park – part of Swansea's golden jubilee celebrations – and Brynmelyn Park had opened. Unlike its predecessors, Victoria Park was typically used for sporting activity and was a key venue for league rugby and soccer. It was also to house the memorial to the South African War of 1899-1902 (until the construction of the new Guildhall in the 1930s necessitated its removal) and the statue of William Thomas.

Successful provision of parks near the town centre was, however, matched by significant delays in providing facilities in the crowded, working-class parts of Swansea on the east bank of the river Tawe. It ought to have been relatively straightforward. The need for open spaces was recognised by both council and landowner, and the Earl of Jersey — the principal landowner in St Thomas — made a gift of land in 1885. Unfortunately for Swansea Corporation, the Local Government Board was unwilling to sanction a loan to construct the roads and sewers that the Earl

This postcard, dating from 1907, shows the entrance to Victoria Park as it was prior to the construction of the Guildhall. In the background is Swansea's Boer War memorial, which was unveiled on 15 April 1904. The statue was removed to its present location overlooking Mumbles Road in the early 1930s.

requested as part of the deal.[20] In their letter to the corporation, the Board observed that:

In the neighbourhood in which the ground is situate there is at present a sufficiency of areas not occupied by buildings, so that there is no want of air space or danger of crowding too many dwellings within narrow limits, while the sea is described as being not far distant.[21]

Unable to afford to spend money on building the infrastructure demanded by the Jersey Estate, it took until 1902 for Jersey Park to open.

Undeterred by the difficulties faced in St Thomas, William Thomas continued to press for more facilities across Swansea. He earned the ire of his colleagues in the town hall, including the clerk of the council who went so far as to remark that 'the lungs of Swansea [are] to no inconsiderable extent provided for'. Thomas, however, believed that the corporation were sacrificing noble principles in order to fill 'landlords' pockets'.[22] Such a debate would eventually rage in most towns when the question of providing public parks arose. Councils needed land to lay out new facilities and that meant making deals with landlords often on favourable terms to the estates. Gifts of land for parks, therefore, came with the proviso of public expenditure on new roads, sewers, and other essential infrastructure.

Gifted by Lord Tredegar to the people of Cardiff in December 1901, Splott Park developed quickly in the years before the Great War. The bandstand opened in 1904, the bowling green in 1906 and the tennis courts in 1907. The open-air swimming pool, visible in the centre of this photograph taken by the RAF in July 1950, opened on 14 August 1922 and was converted for indoor use in the mid-1970s.

This was especially true in Cardiff. Roath Park, which opened in 1894 and was the first municipal park in the city, is often remembered as a munificent gift from the Bute Estate and the Tredegar Estate. In practice, however, philanthropic benevolence in providing valuable open spaces was motivated also by the prospect, largely at the city's expense, of improving the rental income from the houses that looked onto Roath Park — hence

the annoyance of those who moved into the area believing it to be leafy and upmarket only to discover that the park attracted all sorts of people, including the wrong ones. As one correspondent complained in the *Western Mail*:

I would call the attention of all concerned to the scandalous manner in which gangs of local "hooligans" are allowed after dark to congregate upon and around the seats, for choice those nearest the houses facing the park, and howl obscene songs, some of which to accentuate the grievance are set to well-known hymn tunes [...] Talk about a few dogs howling – bah![23]

When Cardiff Corporation took control of the land in the late 1880s, it was boggy and difficult to make use of. Its poor quality, particularly at the recreation ground, would be a recurring problem for decades, whether it was blamed on heavy rain and generally wet conditions as was suggested in the late 1890s when residents complained or, following attempts to level the site in the early 1920s, on the stench of rotting household refuse. The latter effort proved a breeding ground for large flies (described as being like mosquitoes) and a lingering smell in the vicinity of the park. 'To allow our young people to play on top of such a putrid heap', complained the *Cardiff and Suburban News* in 1924,

'is a disgrace to the city'.[24] So bad was the situation that a local residents' association known grandly as the Roath Park Health Protection Committee was formed to pressure the city authorities into sorting out the ground once and for all.[25]

Roath Park, with its large gardens and boating lake cost Cardiff Corporation tens of thousands of pounds to lay out, largely because of the costs of transforming what was essentially waste ground into a useable public park. Initial estimates produced in January 1888 were set at a conservative £30,000. Within a month they had risen to £50,000, at which point councillors began verbally attacking each other. Fred Beavan accused his brother Ebenezer, the chair of the parks committee, of wanting to spend £100,000 in a wasteful turn of opulence. Others complained that the park was just for the benefit of Roath Ward and one even went so far as to suggest that 'they were making a great mistake'. At the end of the meeting, it was resolved to stick to the initial

The lake in Roath Park quickly became a hive of leisure activity ranging from rowboats to swimming and diving. As with promenading, boating was very much something to be seen doing and people dressed up accordingly.

estimates despite Ebenezer Beavan's warning that this would render the park 'a dry, barren wilderness with nothing but bridges, fences and roads'.[26] It eventually cost £55,000.

Building work took several years to complete and councillors would taunt each other in council meetings asking when it would open. In March 1893, for example, the chairman of the parks committee promised that 'the day of opening would probably be some time before the millennium [but] probably not this side of Christmas'.[27] In the event, the park opened in the summer of 1894 and was marked by a great procession of dignitaries through the centre of Cardiff followed by representatives of the trade unions,

20 June 1894: opening day for Roath Park! With bunting and flags flying across the town, the unveiling of new civic amenities was a major event marked by the whole community. Notice the horse-drawn floats carrying local dignitaries and the marching banners of local churches, chapels and trades unions.

local companies, and voluntary organisations, all marching behind their banners. The pomp and ceremony of the day was quite apparent, with the Union flag flying from many a town-centre window. The opening of a public park, then as now, was a major public event.

Roath Park was almost a triumph: its large botanic gardens, sizeable boating lake with diving platforms and launching stages, and recreation ground for the playing of sport, made for an attractive and multi-purpose leisure amenity. That was, of course, if you could get there. Little more than a fortnight after the grand opening by the Earl of Dumfries on 20 June 1894, a letter appeared in the *Western Mail* making the simple observation that 'if the whole of the inhabitants of Cardiff and neighbourhood are to have an opportunity of visiting the Roath Park, it is necessary that some quicker mode of conveyance should be established than at present exists'.[28] At the time of unveiling, Roath Park was some distance from the nearest train station or tramline, which made travel from western and southern parts of the town such as Grangetown, Canton and Butetown much more difficult, with only horse-drawn buses providing public transport to the park.

By September of that year, the debate focused on access to the park on Sundays and the provision of buses for working people to be able to make use of it. 'Not one third of the population of Cardiff attend a place of worship', contended one councillor, 'but if the buses and trams ran on a Sunday [...] these people might go out to the Roath Park and enjoy God's fresh air, which was infinitely better than remaining in the vitiated atmosphere of a small room and reading novels or newspapers'.[29] Voices of opposition were raised from across the political spectrum, including the emerging Labour movement whose representatives argued that 'it is the wish of the Labour section to do away with all Sunday work of whatever description'. In the event the vote failed but the question of access did not disappear. Before the end of the decade, the council relented and the tramways corporation began operating services in the direction of Roath Park, which were regularly full and proved the popularity of Sunday in the park.[30]

In a short time following the opening of Roath Park, towns across Wales began to take seriously for the first time the provision of public open space. In communities such as Abertillery, Cardigan, Carmarthen, Mountain Ash, Neath and Newport there

was to be a public park opened before the turn of the century (typically to mark the Diamond Jubilee in 1897) and in Aberdare, Cardiff and Swansea the network of facilities was extended further. Bellevue Park in Newport was amongst the grandest of these. Opened by the Mayor, Frank Phillips, on 8 September 1894, the park had been laid out to a design by Thomas Mawson.[31] Born in Lancashire in 1861, Mawson gained an international reputation for his park designs and published several key texts on the subject including *The Art and Craft of Garden Making* (1901). Featuring entrance lodges, bandstand, a waterfall, terraced gardens leading to a fine arts and crafts pavilion, and even a children's playground equipped with swings and roundabouts, Bellevue was a park that encompassed both the Victorian notions of rational recreation and a freer sense of play. More formal sporting facilities followed in the Edwardian period, with bowling greens in 1904 and tennis courts in 1907, both the result of public appeals.[32]

Owning a public park was a considerable source of civic pride and came to be seen as an indicator of a responsible, grown-up community. For Cardiff, there was great pressure to prove itself to be the leading town in Wales in all areas of public and commercial life. Following the unveiling of Victoria Park, Canton, in 1897, the editor of the *Western Mail* opined that with the two parks in its possession, its rivals had been left behind. 'Like the greatest town in Wales, as it is', the paper argued, 'Cardiff very appropriately enjoys a pre-eminence, among other things, in the matter of public parks, which entitles it to stand side-by-side with such places as Manchester and Birmingham, Liverpool, Sheffield and Leeds'.[33] Further praise was forthcoming from the trade journal *Gardeners' Chronicle*, which labelled Cardiff as 'one of the most progressive of provincial towns'.[34]

Local rivalries came to be expressed as much through the size and grandeur of public facilities as they did through sporting contests. This was particularly true of the decades' old battle between Aberdare and Merthyr Tydfil, but equally applied to the tussle between Wrexham and Llangollen for pre-eminence in the north-east and that between Bangor and Caernarfon in the north-west.[35] For Aberdare, the push to provide a public park in the 1860s was a key part of its progressive identity. Considering itself to be at the forefront of Welsh civilisation in the middle part of the nineteenth century, the town was heralded by contemporaries as the 'Athens of Wales', a tribute to its

A respite amidst industrialism and dense housing, Bellevue Park was Newport's first municipal open space. This photograph, taken by Aerofilms in 1929, shows it in its interwar heyday. As with all parks, Bellevue has continued to evolve and became home to the town's first adventure playground in the 1970s.

attachment to rationalism, liberalism and nonconformity. In providing a park in 1869, Aberdare had done much to distance itself from its arguably more violent, dirty and poorly-governed neighbour: Merthyr Tydfil.

Aberdare Park was laid out on a part of Hirwaun Common originally set aside for public use by the Inclosure Commissioners in 1857. Landscaping work began in 1866 and the park was opened to the public three years later at a cost of £5,000. This

The first genuinely municipal park in the south Wales valleys, Aberdare Park was a beacon of rational recreation and a triumph for the town's liberal-minded middle classes who believed it a fitting facility for the Athens of Wales. By the time this photograph was taken in 1929, it had developed to include an open-air swimming pool (opened in June 1902), tennis courts and bowling green.

was borrowed against the rates and paid back by the local board (and its successors) over the course of the next thirty years. Thus, by the time of the Diamond Jubilee in 1897, the people of Aberdare owned their park outright and had only to pay the

annual cost of maintenance. Although situated in the more fashionable part of the town, in keeping with Victorian parks of this kind, it gave to Aberdare an aura of difference. 'I was projected into a new world', recalled Edmund Stonelake of his journey from

Pontlottyn to Aberdare to live, 'I found myself in a far brighter physical and cultural environment'.[36] The contrast with those communities that did not have public parks was increasingly stark. Stonelake observes in his autobiography that in Pontlottyn 'there were no playing fields for children or adults [...] the word amenities social or otherwise was not part of our language'.[37] The 'muddy roads' were the poor substitute for green grass and maintained playgrounds. Things were little better in neighbouring Rhymney where Thomas Jones was born. What passed for a park in Rhymney – the grounds of Rhymney House – was reserved for the privileged use of the ironmasters. 'On one day in the year', Jones wrote in the *Times* in the 1930s, 'were we allowed to file past them in a Sunday school procession through the park'.[38] The war memorial park, which became the main park for Rhymney and Pontlottyn, was not opened until May 1925.[39]

The longest and saddest battle for a public park took place in Merthyr Tydfil. Unlike the progressively independent Aberdare Local Board of Health, Merthyr's local board was controlled by the ironmasters. They were reluctant to spend their own money or revenues from the public purse to improve the town, or to release land in the constricted surroundings of their works, and Merthyr suffered from the want of public facilities until late in the nineteenth century when the influence of the 'ironocracy' broke down. As such, would-be reformers were prevented from utilising the mechanisms of local government to effect social change and were forced to develop alternative channels: newspapers such as the *Merthyr Telegraph* and institutions such as the Merthyr Chamber of Trade. Through these, liberal-minded citizens were able to campaign for and occasionally seek to provide public facilities including recreational amenities. Merthyr, complained David Evans a local auctioneer in the 1870s, has 'no hospital, no place of recreation or amusement, no charities, no town hall, no public library, and no reading room!'[40] It was a sad indictment of Merthyr's lack of civic progress despite having been Wales' largest town for decades.

In 1881, in an effort to overcome the lack of a park, a local solicitor by the name of Frank James put forward a proposal to convert part of the Thomastown tips into a small recreation ground.[41] Notable for its emphasis on soccer and cricket facilities rather than the gentle public walks and shrubberies that were more typical of Victorian parks, the proposals were also remarkably cheap — a result of the initiative being undertaken by the chamber of trade, which could not raise revenues from the rates. Final estimates produced in the summer of 1881 projected expenditure on the ground of just £375.[42] Unfortunately for the liberal proponents, the landowners — represented by the local MP Charles Herbert James — felt unable to provide a lease longer than twenty-one years, which the chamber of trade argued was insufficient, and so negotiations fell apart.[43]

The collapse of the negotiations was a shock to the members of the chamber of trade and remained a sore issue over the course of the next few years, particularly during the Golden Jubilee of 1887. The *Merthyr Express* complained of being without 'one inch of ground for pleasure or recreation, without a mayor or corporation, without a town hall, a theatre, public baths, or indeed any public building of any kind worthy of the name'. It was, the paper concluded, 'symptomatic of the town's insistent slide into backwardness'.[44] Worse, was the belief (and fear) that 'we shall be left behind by our neighbours at Aberdare if we do not look out and act'.[45] Dulled by the consistent failure to achieve incorporation as a borough (a level of government thought to befit Merthyr's size), the campaign for a public park lapsed until the Diamond Jubilee of 1897 prompted a renewal of efforts. David Davies, a local councillor in Merthyr, captured the mood of resignation when he reflected that 'Merthyr [is] a long way behind the spirit of the age'.[46]

By that time, local government changes in 1894 had replaced the local board of health with Merthyr Tydfil Urban District Council and whilst many of the same problems of having wards operating as the pocket franchises of the ironmasters still existed, the emphasis of local government had shifted towards greater outlay on public amenities. The Diamond Jubilee was to prove the catalyst, as in many other local authorities, for a public park. Preferring gifts of land to the complex process, not to mention cost, of direct purchase from a landowner, the council wrote to several individuals across the district to solicit interest. In the end, they received offers from just two of the ten estates approached: Thomastown tips and some land at Treharris. Since Treharris was not central enough, the council accepted the offer of Thomastown and took possession in 1898. The park eventually opened five years later at a cost of £5,000.[47] In an effort to compensate for decades of neglect, Thomastown Park provided for physical recreation with its tennis courts, bowling green, and children's playground as well as the more typical botanic gardens and bandstand. It also served as the location for Merthyr's memorial to the dead of the South African War. Thomastown was an orthodox public park in the sense that its primary clientele was middle class. Situated to the east of the town centre in an area of affluent housing near to the synagogue and local infirmary, it was 'the first exclusively residential area to be created by those at the top stratum of Merthyr's population'.[48] Like the Common in Pontypridd and Cwmdonkin in Swansea all those years before, this was a park designed with the middle classes in mind.

Rest and Play

Victorian public parks dominate the lists of parks and gardens registered by Cadw, English Heritage, and Historic Scotland. Recognition of the integral aesthetic qualities of parks is understandable but their role as workhorses is less widely recognised. Sophia Gardens, for all its impressive character, was the bedrock of league sport in Cardiff: every weekend and during the mid-week half-day, scores of teams made use of every part of the grounds for rugby, soccer, baseball, and cricket. Members of clubs often had to turn up outside the gates before dawn to stake a claim to their pitch. Victoria Park served a similar function for Swansea from the 1880s onwards.

The rise to prominence of organised sporting activity challenged the perception of parks as stately places of 'keep off the grass' signs and of notice boards that forbade a host of activities from kicking a ball to taking cuttings. 'Was it essential that £1,200 should be expended in making a carriage drive?' enquired one resident of Aberdare in 1869, 'was it necessary to spend £1,200 in planting ornamental trees, £500 in ornamental ponds, and £800 in two lodges?' Contemporaries recognised that Aberdare Park and others like it, for all their significance and aesthetic interest, were spaces designed for one class of people but paid for in the name of another. The critic from Aberdare continued: 'The working man is fully aware that the park is not for his benefit'.[49] By the Edwardian period, this had begun to change as public parks increasingly became spaces that accepted and incorporated sport rather than prohibiting it, though they remained locations of more serene forms of leisure such as promenading or drinking tea at the refreshment pavilion.

The shift from a predominantly middle-class space to one catering for working-class recreation took place in the first decade of the twentieth century. It was signalled in parks such as that at Abertillery, which from the outset had open-air swimming baths alongside the bandstand and landscaped gardens.[50] Eventually sporting facilities came to dominate at Abertillery, with the remarkable oval-shaped rugby ground, cricket pitch, and tennis courts all developed shortly after the Great War. The changing nature of public parks was registered by designers and parks managers and much discussed in trade journals. The Superintendent of Parks for Cardiff, William Wallace Pettigrew, wrote a series of articles in the *Gardeners' Chronicle* in 1907

For most of the fifty years before the Great War, one family became synonymous with public parks, private gardens and recreation grounds in and around Cardiff: the Pettigrews. Their expertise was regularly called upon by local councils when developing their own parks. This photograph shows (from left to right) William Wallace Pettigrew, Andrew Pettigrew, Andrew Alexander Pettigrew and Hugh Allan Pettigrew.

outlining the changes taking place in the city. 'People', he wrote, 'will not visit these parks simply for the sake of getting a breath of fresh air'. Whilst recognising that 'parks are made as beautiful as possible', since this was a helpful inducement, Pettigrew also made the case for provision to be made 'for the enjoyment of all kinds of games and sports'.[51]

1907 was not the year when the aesthetics of garden design gave way to rowdy rugby fans and the referee's whistle but Pettigrew was writing on the cusp of significant changes in what, and for whom, public parks should be. In that vein he noted the change to a system of pitch permits in the city, which made the flow of sports matches much more effective. It was no longer practical for teams to nominate someone to wait outside the park gates at dawn to lay claim to a playing field for the day. As if to prove him right, over the course of the first year of operation, some 2,000 pitch permits were issued to clubs in Cardiff.[52]

In such a world, parks administrators turned to a fairly ruthless method of space allocation: if a particular sport was not being played often enough then it was erased from the landscape of the park and the area was given over to further playing fields for soccer, rugby, cricket, or, in towns in the valleys and along the south-east coast, baseball. During the Great War, for example, the numbers playing cricket in Swansea collapsed and with the continued rise of junior soccer placing pressure on the number of pitches available, parks managers exchanged several cricket pitches for soccer ones.[53] Quite unlike in the Victorian period, then, parks in the first years of the twentieth century were altered to suit the recreational needs of people rather than prescribing particular forms of leisure.

The progression had been a chaotic one. Following the opening of Aberdare Park, a correspondent of the *Aberdare Times* pondered the question of allowing cricket to be played and concluded that 'a game [...] would be for less than a hundred and annoy a thousand'.[54] Aberdare cricket club was granted use of the park only to find themselves ejected two years later to make room for the local rifle club.[55] This mixed attitude to sporting activity within public parks and gardens was also evident in Cardiff in the 1890s. At Plasturton Gardens, for example, the simple, continuous grass plot that had originally formed the site was criticised by councillors for being 'open to all manner of rough and bad-mannered children' and so it was decided to redesign

the layout and to separate out sections of the lawns with flower beds and gravel walks in order to curb the playing of football and 'other rough games' and 'bad language'. At Despenser Gardens, Riverside Lawn Tennis Club was permitted to use the lawns for their matches but councillors refused to grant exclusive access for fear of limiting the recreational opportunities of local children.[56]

In districts that were not blessed with public parks, such as the Rhondda valleys and Merthyr, the Victorian conception of a public park remained strong even on the eve of the Great War. When Gelli Park was opened in July 1912, local newspapers greeted it as a sign of the transformation of the area, which had 'the reputation some years ago of being the worst part of the Rhondda'.[57] The same was desired of Treharris, which also gained its first park in 1912. Covering 18 acres and situated on the mountainside above the village, the park initially lacked any formal facilities for recreation save a bandstand (as was the case at Gelli Park). Bowling greens, tennis courts, and a children's playground would follow in later years.

The culmination of these shifting attitudes to the place of sporting activity in public parks lies in the plans for open spaces created in the years just prior to the outbreak of the Great War. In the case of the Ynysangharad Fields in Pontypridd, the early designs for their transformation into a park, drawn in about 1909, show that the predominant purpose was to be sport rather than promenading amongst the flowers. It catered for several different forms of sport and the ornamental features were kept to a minimum. Though this idea was altered by the time the park came to be laid out in the 1920s, not least because of a paddling pool and lido being built on the site of the planned tennis courts, sport remained an essential part of the design.

The same is true of Bellevue Park in Wrexham, which stands as the finest example of a late-Edwardian park in Wales. Purchased from Lady Williams Wynn in 1907 at a cost of almost £4,350, the land — designated by Wrexham Corporation as 'y parciau' — was transformed into a public park according to a design entitled 'Erica', the winning entry in a public competition organised by the council in 1909. The layout incorporated bowling greens, a soccer pitch, large lawns, tree-lined avenues, and the ever-popular bandstand. Whilst the main body of the park opened in 1910, elements had their own unveiling ceremonies: the children's

By the early part of the twentieth century, the estates of the ironmasters in towns such as Merthyr Tydfil had been taken over for popular recreation. This Edwardian postcard shows the boating lake in Cyfarthfa Park. The castle behind, once the home of the Crawshay Family, was transformed into a school and museum.

playground in 1913, the bowling greens and the bandstand in 1914, and the pavilion and four grass tennis courts in 1915.[58]

For Merthyrians, the Edwardian decade was one of transformation. Social and cultural infrastructure that had been needed since the 1850s such as a town hall and public library had been constructed and now the local authority actively sought to create open spaces, seeking to reverse the blackening of nearly a century of industrialisation. Thomastown Park had proved a success but it was both too small to cater for the entire town and not grand enough to stand as the showpiece for Merthyr's new-found civic pride. The solution came when the Corporation was approached to purchase Cyfarthfa Castle and its grounds from the Crawshay estate. The sale was completed in 1909 for

Shaped by the growing tolerance of sport in public parks before the Great War, Wrexham's Belle Vue has an abundance of football pitches, tennis courts, bowling greens and free open space. The bandstand, once the centrepiece of public parks, has been relegated to a quiet corner and the tree-lined pathways kept to a minimum.

the sum of £19,700. Nearly 160 acres of parkland, woodland, lakes, and the mansion house itself were now in the council's possession. F.T. James, a councillor for the Park ward in the north-west of the town, summed up much local opinion: 'the money spent on the park was one of the finest investments they [...] could make'.[59] Cyfarthfa Park soon had bowling greens, tennis courts, a boat house, a tea chalet and a bandstand to emphasise its status as one of the largest public parks in Wales.

By the outbreak of the Great War, then, the public park had begun the process of transformation from an aesthetic environment to a place of physical recreation. As parks developed they increasingly included features such as bowling greens, tennis courts, and relatively spacious playing fields. In the years after the war this process would continue with the concept of the public park being radically altered and sporting activity coming to dominate. Despite the economic hardships of the inter-war years, this was to be a golden age with more public parks, playing fields, recreation grounds and children's playgrounds in more communities than in any earlier period.

Even as parks evolved as places of sport and pleasure, their role as a refuge from the hustle and bustle of town life remained constant. The contrast between Pontypridd's busy town centre with its railway station, shops and cinemas, and the tranquillity of the park is apparent in this photography from 1955.

The combination of local government and charitable organisations transformed the number of playing fields and parks in the 1920s and 1930s. The legacy of those years remains at the heart of the sporting environment in the twenty-first century. Attention is often given to the beauty of Victorian and Edwardian parks with their bandstands and finely planted gardens, but without the hardships, sacrifices and willing effort of those men, women and children who lived through the 1920s and 1930s, many communities would not have had a park, recreation ground or children's playground until after the Second World War. The inter-war period is rightly remembered as years of great suffering — the 'locust years' as Gwyn Alf Williams once described them — but this was also a time of great vision and achievement, of which the sporting environment inherited by subsequent generations is but one reminder.

Post-War Playing Fields

In comparison with the 1920s and 1930s, the post-war period — at least until the 1960s — was marked by stagnation and lack of investment aside from a brief flurry in the first years of the 1945–51 Labour governments. Many communities still made use of facilities laid out during the financial difficulties of the inter-war years but few, given post-war fiscal turmoil, could afford to offer modern amenities like those slowly being built elsewhere in the country and at a rather more dramatic pace in continental Europe. In a report published in 1963, the Central Council of Physical Recreation (CCPR) for Wales observed that there was a 'grave shortage of playing fields'.[83] The county development plans, which local authorities were compelled to draw together following Labour's Town and Country Planning Act of 1947, had begun to shed a great deal of light on the state of public open spaces and the inequalities in provision for recreation and leisure right across Wales.

Most county surveyors shared the view of the borough engineer of Swansea, R.D. Moody, who wrote in his 1955 report

Gwernifor Park was one of a series of new facilities laid out by Mountain Ash Urban District Council after the Second World War. Badly affected by unemployment and outmigration in the 1930s, these amenities offered hope for a better future.

that 'there are many deficiencies in the present distribution of open space, and in particular, a lack of a sufficient number of playing fields'.[84] Expectations of where parks should be located, particularly in cities, were changing and historic imbalances such as inadequate provision in inner city areas were noted amidst a general belief that there were not enough. Even towns and cities that had a relatively good record of laying out public parks and playing fields fell behind national targets. In comparison to the National Playing Fields Association's 'five-acre standard' — that is, 5 acres of open space per 1,000 of the population with at least 3 acres reserved for sport. Cardiff was far behind in 1945 with a standard of just 1.95 acres. By contrast cities in the North of England such as Leeds and Sheffield (at 6.5 acres and 5.75 acres respectively) were ahead of national standards and provided models of best practice.[85]

The city authorities in Cardiff, however, had wide-ranging ambitions for the transformation of public leisure available to residents and tourists alike. In a report to the parks committee of Cardiff Council in February 1948, the recreation organiser, Tom Davies, drew attention to what he perceived to be Cardiff's needs: 'two hundred soccer pitches, 100 baseball, 100 cricket, 50 rugby, 50 hockey, 20 lacrosse, 20 basketball, 20 netball, 20 squash, 20 badminton, 150 outdoor tennis, 48 indoor tennis, 144 outdoor bowling rinks, 24 indoor bowling rinks, one swimming bath for every 30,000 of the population, one athletic and cycle track for every 50,000 of the population and one skating track for every 50,000'.[86] Judging by statistics published in December 2009, these projections have yet to be met (although circumstances of active participation in sport are somewhat different in twenty-first century Britain): today Cardiff has 134 soccer pitches, 45 rugby pitches, 39 baseball diamonds, 16 cricket pitches, and 53 tennis courts, but the population of the city is over 25 per cent bigger than in 1948.

In Newport, the situation was little better. In the early 1950s, the town had a population of around 105,000 and was Wales's third largest. In many ways, the provision of public parks and playing fields was still reflective of earlier patterns of construction: more generous in outer districts and more restricted in central areas. With a total of around 340 acres of open space or 3.2 acres per 1,000 people, the borough fell short of the 5-acre standard and the council's self-imposed aspiration of 7 acres. Most of this

Maindy Stadium, which opened in May 1951, was the culmination of nearly three decades of struggle to provide a world-class cycling and athletics venue in Cardiff. Originally intended to be the focal point of the 1958 Empire Games, it was considered too small and the games were held in the Arms Park instead.

space was devoted to parkland and playgrounds and sport in Newport's parks was relatively limited with just eight of the forty-five sites providing playing fields. This translated into eighteen soccer pitches, seven rugby pitches, nine baseball pitches, fourteen cricket pitches, and lesser provision for hockey and netball.

Swansea also suffered from many of the same pressures on its public space although its total available space for recreation and leisure was significantly more generous than either Cardiff or Newport with nearly 720 acres. As had been the case since Victorian times, the eastern half of the city had fewer amenities than did the western half and the undulating nature of the landscape in Swansea made the laying out of playing fields much more difficult than in Cardiff. Post-war planning encouraged further improvements in the provision for districts east of the river Tawe, though the imbalance between east and west remains to this day.

Despite the pressure on space, the facilities available in south Wales were relatively luxurious and generous compared with the situation in mid and north Wales. Merioneth, which provided one of the three case studies for the CCPR report in 1963 (along with Newport and Aberdare) was typical of the central and north-western counties in lacking parks and playing fields. 'Most villages have one soccer pitch', observed the authors, '[which] is often provided by the enterprise of the local clubs' although some were 'simply sawdust-marked pitches on grazing land'.[87] Montgomeryshire, with larger communities such as Newtown, Llanidloes and Machynlleth, provided facilities that were better, though still far from comprehensive. During the Second World War, the Montgomery County Recreation Association explained to reconstruction planners that:

Comparatively few playgrounds are available. Youth in the countryside has little opportunity for organised games, once he or she has left school. It is often remarked that the country lad does not want games after his day's work, but "out of season" football when the long evenings arrive, is a feature of the Montgomeryshire countryside. Such activity is made possible by the good-will of a local farmer.

Over the course of the second half of the twentieth century, towns in mid and north Wales began to seek the same kinds of facilities available in urbanised areas and the farmer's field became increasingly redundant as a location for sport and recreation. 'Now that the countryman has some leisure' explained David Caradog Jones, then Labour's parliamentary candidate for Montgomeryshire, in 1954, 'he wants all the amenities available to those who live in towns'. This meant parks and cinemas as much as electric lighting, cars, and eventually televisions, though individual facilities such as bowling greens and tennis courts had existed for several decades. Some of the new parks, such as Dolerw Park in Newtown, covered a large area providing not only

for organised sport but also for the more Victorian styles of recreation.

Playgrounds of Adventure

The park continued to be transformed as a public space. New forms of urban planning that followed reconstruction programmes of the 1940s and the county development plans of the 1950s encouraged local authorities to catalogue what was available and think about what improvements could and should be made. Equally significant was the spread of new ideas about recreation such as the adventure playgrounds movement, which began in Denmark in the 1930s and made its way to Britain in the late 1940s: first to London and then to other major cities.[88]

Adventure playgrounds made use of the immediate urban environment. Just as opening up Victorian public parks to organised sporting activity had contributed to the redefinition of 'people's parks', the adventure playground movement sought to reorient the playground to the more anarchic, unstructured tendencies of children at play. The principal aim was to provide a safe place in which children could shape the landscape themselves as they played making use of boxes, tyres, tubing, and other resources that were provided. This reflected a more institutionalised form of traditional practices: children living in towns and cities across Britain often made carts using old boxes and scrapped wheels.

For all their focus on unstructured play, adventure playgrounds were often carefully managed and supported by local authorities. At the forefront of the movement was the Voluntary Community Service in Cardiff, which helped to set up Wales' first adventure playground in Butetown in the late 1960s. Most of Newport's adventure playground, for example, which was managed by the Newport Adventure Playgrounds Association (formed in 1970), was located at the southern edge of Bellevue Park overlooking the railway line and part of the town's industrial zone.

In more recent years, the adventure playground has become an even more formal and traditional leisure environment with fixed facilities. Nevertheless, the connection between the adventure playground and deprivation remains very strong and this is evident in the location of Wales' remaining sites: Llanrumney, Ely and Riverside in Cardiff and Rhyl, which was awarded nearly £170,000 from Sport Wales in 2006 to refurbish

With the rise of seaside tourism along the north Wales coast, swimming baths became part and parcel of the facilities on offer to, and expected by, visitors. This photograph, taken by Aerofilms in 1934, shows the proximity of the baths in Rhos-on-Sea to other typical seaside amenities including Rhos Pier.

and a half from the centre of Wrexham. In an era when walking was the primary mode of transport for most people, the journey to and from the pool took up a relatively large portion of an individual's free time. Attendances at the baths were, as a result, relatively modest. Out of a total population of nearly 7,000, monthly patronage at the baths ranged from 280 people in July to around 70 in the chilly autumnal waters of October. Most of these patrons were children.[6]

This photograph, taken by Royal Commission photographer Dylan Roberts at Llanelli Docks in 1970, shows that diving into and swimming in rivers, canals and docks by no means died away after the provision of leisure centres and public swimming baths.

The Llwyn Onn baths opened on 1 June 1854 and provided two sessions per day at varying costs. Entry between 6am and 10am cost 3*d* with a towel included. The evening session between 6pm and 9pm cost just 1*d* but patrons had to bring their own towels.[7] Moderately popular with local residents, the baths enjoyed the custom of local schools and the military garrison (which paid a monthly subscription of £7), adding greatly to their financial viability. Despite this, the baths closed after just four years

to the lament of the local newspaper, which complained that 'we are left entirely to our odious pools'.[8] Reflecting on his experience of operating baths two decades later, Hugh Davies insisted that only the state could provide swimming baths because the length of time they took to become profitable made them an unattractive proposition to businessmen. With the reluctance of the local council to spend money on baths, no new swimming pool opened in Wrexham until the Tuttle Street Baths in 1901.

For over four decades, Wrexham had 'neither public baths, canal, stream, or body of water of any kind at all suitable for the purpose of ablution'.[9]

For the most part, of course, people went swimming in canals, streams, rivers, and lakes. In Merthyr and Aberdare, the various small ponds dotted around the town centre that were used for ice skating in the winter months provided opportunities for swimming in the spring and summer. In Cardiff, similarly, the Glamorganshire Canal offered plenty of opportunity for residents of several of the town's districts, as did the rivers Taff and Ely. Swansea, with its long beach, was popular with tourists from industrial towns such as Merthyr as residents went bathing in the waters of Oystermouth Bay. In the emerging coastal resorts of north and mid Wales, more formal (but often tidal) facilities were provided by entrepreneurs, including the Siliwen Baths at Bangor.

Swimming in public was not welcomed by everyone: motivated by health concerns or questions of public morality, bathing in canals and rivers was criticised in the newspapers particularly since it often exposed naked bodies to the general public. 'Anyone entering […] these open sewers, as they have been called', complained one correspondent of the *Glamorgan Free Press* 'cannot screen himself from public view, so that it is clearly his duty not to go into the water at all'.[10] Even swimming in the sea was liable to cause moral outrage, as residents of Porthcawl discovered. At a meeting of Porthcawl Urban District Council in July 1912, the beach inspector reported that several male members of the public had fallen into the habit of sitting on the benches overlooking the sands 'to watch ladies undressing and bathing'. These men apparently used binoculars to enhance their view. In an attempt to get their own back, a group of women began insisting on sitting near the men's section of the beach as the men were getting changed to go swimming.[11]

Encouraging would-be swimmers to make use of formal facilities rather than swimming in rivers and canals was the primary challenge of both public and private proprietors of baths. In certain cases, innovative businessmen simply made use of already-existing locations and ensured that they remained visually similar to natural sites. A good example of this phenomenon was the original open-air swimming baths at Gwaunfarren in Merthyr Tydfil. Opened in 1890 by John Vaughan, a local solicitor, they cost nearly £1,600 to build and were set into the hillside amidst sheltering trees and bushes. Fed by a channel off the neighbouring weir and with wooden decking along the pool's edge, the baths were essentially the maintained equivalent of swimming in one of the nearby ponds, albeit far safer. Soon after the baths opened Merthyr Tydfil Swimming Club was founded (it remains in existence) and the baths were regularly used for swimming galas and other aquatic competitions throughout the 1890s.

In Cardiff, the challenge was not successfully met until the rebuilding and roofing of the Corporation Baths in the mid-1890s. Prior to that date, the Guildford Crescent baths, opened on 1 May 1862, had left much to be desired. They included both first-class and second-class baths, a Turkish bath, a cold-water plunge pool for the use of the local Jewish population and a short-lived gymnasium. It was later removed because of the noise. Promoted by its owners as the cleaner, safer alternative to swimming in the canal and local rivers, the baths were in actual fact filled with water that flowed into the first-class pool from a culvert in the Bute Docks feed channel running alongside the building. On top of that, smoke and dust belched into the Cardiff air by locomotives running on the Taff Vale Railway waiting at the Taff Vale Station (today's Queen Street Station), and left a thick layer of scum on the water, meaning that even on sunny days the baths were inhospitable. Poorer patrons swimming in the waters of the second-class bath faced an even worse experience because their bath was filled by the overflow from the first-class pool. Patrons were therefore paying to wade through the dirt of wealthier residents. Little wonder, then, that faced with the choice of swimming for free in dirty canal or river water or paying for the same privilege at the baths, most residents kept their pennies in their pockets for other things.

The Guildford Crescent baths closed in 1871 after a series of poor annual returns. In an effort to salvage the baths for the public, the owners offered the purchase option to Cardiff Corporation who initially turned it down since it was clear it could not be run as a going concern. Reluctance was eventually overcome and the baths passed into public ownership in 1873. After minor refurbishment and structural renewal, the baths reopened to the public and remained a limited success — having been left as an open-air facility the same issues that had affected the privately-run baths remained.

Situated on the seafront at Penarth, these Victorian swimming baths (centre, opposite the pier) were filled with saltwater. The largest indoor swimming baths in Wales until the construction of the Empire Pool in 1958, they regularly hosted galas and other competitions much to the annoyance of the grandees of Cardiff.

By the 1880s and 1890s, attitudes towards providing swimming facilities through public finances had begun to change. Following on from the creation of public parks, there was both an upsurge in interest in swimming and other aquatic sports and a new willingness to provide for them. Indeed, in many parts of the country, swimming was actively encouraged and ultimately placed on the school curriculum, although not always for recreation or life-saving purposes: in Swansea, for example, the School Board 'included swimming [...] so that boys took at least one bath a week'.[12] The first major swimming baths of the 1890s were the Stow Hill baths in Newport. Opened officially by the Mayor, Mark Mordey, on 19 June 1890, they were sited on the former reservoir of the Newport & Pilgwenlly Water Works and had both first-class and second-class swimming baths. Each had an entrance of its own. First-class patrons entered through the fine Tudor-style building on Stow Hill itself, whereas less wealthy swimmers went in around the corner in Wesley Place.

Having ensured success in the summer months, from 1891 onwards Newport Corporation began covering the baths in the winter to provide a gymnasium and entertainment hall used for dancing and other public functions. These seasonal changes ensured the long-term survival of the Stow Hill baths. Their opening finally encouraged Cardiff Corporation to act to improve their own facilities in Guildford Crescent and a major programme of rebuilding took place between 1895 and 1896. It saw the conversion of the baths into the indoor facility, which survived until final closure in 1984. The baths were hailed by the Amateur Swimming Association as offering great possibilities for Cardiff to 'become the life and soul of this movement'.[13] Ironically, the council had rebuilt the first-class bath slightly too small to be used for competitive racing and the salt-water baths at Penarth, which had opened in 1885, had to be used instead.

At the other end of Wales, in Wrexham, the decades-long debate about the usefulness and financial viability of swimming baths was coming to an end. Having settled in favour, the council purchased the remains of the Willow Brewery on the corner of Tuttle Street and Willow Street to provide a central location. Following an inquiry in October 1899, into the viability of borrowing £2,000 to cover the costs of the baths, Wrexham Council began building work. Completed by early 1901, the baths opened to great acclaim that summer and were heralded as a major step forward in environmental terms since they were heated by the town's refuse incinerator next door. The Tuttle Street baths were a major fixture in the Wrexham townscape until the 1970s when the construction of a modern leisure centre heralded their closure and subsequent demolition.

Given the relative paucity of swimming baths constructed in Wales before 1900 and the great periods of growth in the inter-war years and in the 1970s, the Edwardian period is easily overlooked, yet it was then that the foundations of a more widespread network of swimming facilities were laid. This is particularly true in the South Wales Coalfield where local councils, under the influence of increasing numbers of Labour members, began to take seriously the matter of recreational provision. The first councils to act were Abertillery Urban District and Margam Urban District in 1900 and they were soon followed by Aberdare Urban District in 1902, Ogmore and Garw Urban District in 1905 and Swansea Borough in 1913. The baths in Abertillery, Aberdare and Swansea were opened in public parks (in the case of Swansea at Morriston Park) and were seen as part of the ongoing development of those facilities. In Ogmore and Garw, however, the swimming baths were independent of other resources. Constructed next to the river in Pontycymer and filled by river water from a culvert, they were subjected to the pollution of the River Garw and thus did not always present the most hospitable conditions for swimmers.

Better experiences could be found in the small number of indoor baths present at several of the workmen's halls and miners' institutes across the coalfield. The most famous of these was the large swimming baths located in the basement of Nixon's Workmen's Hall in Mountain Ash which opened in 1899.[14] They were not an isolated example. The very first swimming baths in the Rhondda, for instance, were located in the workmen's hall in Llwynypia and later there were also swimming baths in the Ferndale and Blaenllechau Workmen's Hall. Elsewhere in the coalfield, there were swimming baths at Aberaman Workmen's Hall, at Powell Tillery Workmen's Hall in Abertillery and at Nine Mile Point Workmen's Hall in Cwmfelinfach. Though not strictly public in the sense of being owned and operated by the local council, these baths were a community-owned resource, precursors of both the pithead baths and the lidos of the 1920s and 1930s.

Workmen's Baths. Llwynypia.

The Llwynypia workmen's baths were situated inside the workmen's hall and were the first swimming baths to be built in the Rhondda. Several miners' institutes had baths, including Nixon's in Mountain Ash and Nine Mile Point Workmen's Hall in Cwmfelinfach, but most found them too expensive to operate.

The Inter-war Boom

Although the 1920s and 1930s in Wales will forever be linked to unemployment, hardship and industrial action, they were also years of significant change in the urban environment: new public parks, welfare grounds, housing estates and swimming baths were built. Increases in the provision of all of these came in response to the need to stimulate the economy and many were funded through special initiatives linked to the direct amelioration of unemployment. In 1918, the much-delayed Carnegie Trust report into the provision of swimming baths and wash-houses across the United Kingdom was published and detailed, for the first time, the record of every part of the country. There were clear successes in England and central Scotland but weak provision in the rest of Scotland, in Ireland and in Wales. Just a handful of local authorities — almost all concentrated in the urban districts of south Wales — had constructed swimming baths of their own. Most were open-

air and built in the Edwardian decade. Just four indoor swimming pools were recorded: those in Wrexham, Cardiff, Penarth and Newport. The pattern in north Wales (aside from Wrexham) already typified later developments: located in seaside towns and resorts, the baths were either tidal or situated near the beach.[15]

Overall, the report noted an absence of swimming baths across mid and west Wales with the emergence of a network of facilities in south Wales and (in more scattered fashion) along the north Wales coast. The figures provided in the report were not entirely accurate as a snapshot of what was then available: they were based on returns gathered before 1914 and not all swimming pools were included. The open-air swimming baths in Abertillery Park were absent from the statistics as were the indoor swimming baths in Aberystwyth and the tidal baths in Bangor. Baths that opened after 1914 such as those in Abersychan were not present either. Nevertheless, the general patterns of greater provision in urban south Wales and the coastal resorts of north Wales remained true right through the inter-war years.

Several reasons account for this dramatic growth: schemes aimed at tackling the severe levels of unemployment by distributing vital funds to the region for public works projects such as parks, roads and swimming baths; the coming to power of the Labour Party at local and national levels with promises to provide much needed leisure amenities and a willingness to spend money on them; and the involvement of charitable organisations such as the Carnegie Trust that undertook to provide finance for

projects that governments could not. Generally, the 1920s and 1930s marked the beginnings of what might be called the cultural welfare state that provided for the entertainment of local people through physical activity and sport, the arts or the cinema.

The period began, however, with dilapidated swimming pools and defunct private investment as a result of four years of war. The Gwaunfarren Baths in Merthyr Tydfil had been neglected since 1914 and the fixtures and fittings — especially the wooden decking — pilfered. What was left was in a serious state of disrepair and closed. In Aberystwyth, too, the Victorian swimming

The Rock Baths were opened in 1938 and funded by the Special Areas Commission. So named because of the Rock Brewery, which occupied the site until the early 1920s, the baths were closed in 1975 by Cynon Valley Borough Council despite local protests.

Barry's Cold Knap Lido opened in 1926 and was constructed by the voluntary labour of the local unemployed. Once one of the largest open-air swimming baths in Britain, it was closed in 1996. This Aerofilms photograph, taken in 1929, shows the baths as they were originally conceived: lacking the semi-circular changing boxes familiar to later swimmers, which were built in 1937, and the post-war children's paddling pool.

baths on Bath Street were actively considered for other purposes and eventually became a cinema in the mid-1920s. Merthyr Tydfil County Borough Council bought the Gwaunfarren site and transformed it into a modern, indoor swimming pool. It opened in 1924 and restored the status of Merthyr as one of the leading aquatic towns in the central valleys of Glamorgan. As bathers in other communities shivered in the cold waters of open-air facilities, those in Merthyr enjoyed the warmth indoors.

The baths that were constructed in this period fulfilled a desire to provide safe, clean facilities that meant children and adults no

longer had to swim in ponds and rivers. In the words of the Chairman of Aberdare Urban District Council, John Lewis, it was time to bring an end to the 'scores of young men and boys [who] were compelled to bathe in local streams made filthy by coal dust because there was no other place for them to go'.[16] In addition, swimming baths were supervised by trained staff and governed by codes of conduct forbidding infractions similar to those that might be the cause of a lifeguard's whistle today. They also provided facilities for diving, water polo and racing competitions. Swimming clubs were quickly established in many communities in

The open-air swimming baths on Rhyl seafront opened in 1930 and were part of a multi-faceted network of leisure amenities along the promenade that aimed at attracting and entertaining tourists in the resort. This photograph, taken by Aerofilms in 1936, shows the baths amidst those facilities and close to the seaside hotels and pier and the town beyond.

this period to take advantage of them and there was an expansion in the uptake of swimming and other water sports for competitive purposes.

For many children, the limitation to this great vision was the cost of using the public pool on a regular basis. Many simply continued to make use of natural places just as they used the streets rather than the supervised public parks. This was particularly true in built-up areas such as central Cardiff. Thomas

Blight, who grew up in Cathays in the inter-war years, remembered 'having learned to swim and dive in the canal'. Only having gained confidence did he progress, along with his friends, to the more formal environment of Roath Park Lake. In nearby Splott, despite the presence of swimming baths, which opened in 1922 in Splott Park, Con O'Sullivan recalled that 'the boys swam wherever they could find water deep enough' and across the city, in the developing suburb of Radyr, boys swam in the quarry pool or in the river Taff.[17] In coastal areas such as Burry Port or Barry, where the sea offered free waters, residents and tourists alike went bathing there instead of at the lidos.[18] 'The sea at Barry', wrote the novelist Walter Haydn Davies in 1972, '[was] clean and frothed by currents, and we headed for it without a thought'.[19]

Nevertheless, seaside towns constructed lidos in the 1920s and 1930s as part of their increasingly sophisticated provision aimed at visitors. The expansive open-air swimming baths at Cold Knap in Barry, which opened on 1 May 1926, were the apex of this movement but were not an isolated example. Across north Wales,

Prestatyn's swimming baths and ballroom opened in 1923. The baths were renovated and renamed the Royal Lido in 1960. Just two years later, on 24 November 1962, the Royal Lido ballroom played host to The Beatles and a crowd that had each paid six shillings to get in.

the tourism industry in towns such as Llandudno, Rhos-on-Sea, Prestatyn and Rhyl received a significant boost from the construction of swimming baths in the inter-war years. In general, seaside lidos were more elaborate in style than the open-air baths found in the South Wales Coalfield and typically took their architectural cues from the art deco movement and maritime themes, rather than the concrete functionalism or pastoral arts and crafts prevalent inland.

The preference for traditional styles inland reflected two key aspects: the origins of many open-air swimming baths in the voluntary labour of unemployed residents and the prevailing arts and crafts form of municipal architecture in south Wales. Voluntary effort was particularly pronounced in the years that followed the Miners' Lockout and General Strike of 1926. In the early 1930s, a group of unemployed in the Carmarthenshire mining village of Hendy undertook to build a swimming pool for the benefit of the local community. Work began in 1932 with the official opening taking place the following year. Fundraising enabled the purchase of materials and the volunteers were paid in kind either with a packet of Woodbine cigarettes (the working-class brand of choice at the time) or a bar of chocolate for the rare volunteer who did not smoke. Unemployed volunteers in nearby Brynamman took heart from the success of the Hendy scheme and built their own baths. These opened in 1934.

In the village of Taff's Well, volunteers transformed the remnants of the Victorian tepid spa into a new open-air swimming baths which opened in the early 1930s. The spa waters at Taff's Well had been in use since Roman times and residents hoped that children would make use of them rather than bathing in the Taff as it bent its way past the village on its journey to the Bristol Channel. The baths had changing boxes along the Pontypridd side and wooden decking along the Cardiff side and the entire facility blended into the wooded, hilly landscape behind. 'Taff's Well baths on a sunny summer's day made Barry Island look as empty as a desert', recalled one resident, 'it was a suntrap and many made use of the sunbathing platform alongside the pool'.[20]

A few miles away, in Pontypridd, two water tanks that had formerly been used by the Rhondda Brewing Company but were, by the early 1930s, lying in a state of disrepair, were transformed into a bathing pool by young volunteers from the St John's Guild Football Club of Graig Street. Loaned tools by the council and given zinc sheets by the brewery, the young people of the Graig created a swimming facility for themselves. Though not remembered or ever recorded as a formal swimming pool, the transformation of the water tanks gained recognition in the local newspaper and was symptomatic of the strong spirit of voluntary action that existed throughout the coalfield. But, as the newspaper reported, without the support of the council, the scheme could never have been brought to a happy, successful conclusion.[21]

Given the cost of building swimming pools — several thousand pounds in the interwar years — they were much less commonly built by volunteers than were recreation grounds and playing fields, which could be laid out over a number of years. The provision by the Miners' Welfare Fund for swimming baths at Wattstown Park, built in the 1920s, or those in Seven Sisters that opened in 1935, was uncommon. The bulk of what was constructed in this period came from local authorities; but without financial assistance from central government schemes such as the Unemployment Grants Committee, the Special Areas Commission, and the Miners' Welfare Fund it is certain that the number of baths would have been far fewer. Such a reality was experienced in north Wales where the limited returns from the Miners' Welfare Fund were concentrated in the coalfield communities of Denbighshire and Flintshire and the entire region lay outside the remit of the Special Areas Commission. Notable successes such as the Buckley baths, which opened in 1928, were thus isolated examples.

Perhaps the finest swimming baths constructed in south Wales, broadly on the basis of money from the Miners' Welfare Fund, was the lido in Ynysangharad Park, which opened in July 1927. Designed by William Lowe, the council surveyor in Pontypridd, the building evoked a Roman villa and the history of Roman bathing through the clever use of Mediterranean red tiling for the roof. Broadly rectangular in shape, the baths were designed with a half-circular shallow end with deeper water in the centre. This provided easy access to the fifty changing boxes that ran along the outer edge of the baths and to the seating area. The fountains that were located in the centre formed part of the pumping system and brought clean, fresh water into the pool. With its great size, the baths were regularly used for aquatic sports including water polo and swimming races and in 1928 Pontypridd Swimming Club was formed.

The lido in Ynysangharad Park is one of the few remaining traces of inter-war provision for public swimming. Constructed in a style that evokes the Roman villas of Tuscany, it was extremely popular and used for all manner of aquatic sports including, as this photograph vividly records, water polo.

Encouraged by the success of the lido in Ynysangharad Park, which opened to much acclaim having been funded through a significant grant from the Miners' Welfare Fund, Rhondda Urban District Council (RUDC) decided to construct a lido of their own. Initial ideas — which included providing baths at Gelligaled Park in Ystrad and at Garth Park in Trealaw — were drawn together by the council surveyor, Eli Taylor, over the course of 1929–30. With external events following the Wall Street Crash of October 1929 overtaking the decision-making process, the plans were dramatically revised in the summer of 1930 as it became apparent the council's finances were increasingly strained by falling income and rising unemployment. In an uncirculated memo, Taylor set out three alternatives with a clear desire to preserve the Gelligaled scheme (including the swimming pool) and the plans for baths at Trealaw were, for the time being, dropped. Even with reduced plans Taylor observed that: 'schemes will have to be completed piece-meal spread over a period of several years as money can be afforded'.[22]

The Gelligaled Baths opened four years later in the summer of 1934 at a cost of £7,200. Although the council sought external support to fund the construction, it was ultimately necessary to fund the project entirely from council revenue. This requirement led to the decision, taken in January 1934, that there would be only one municipal swimming pool for the whole of the Rhondda — any others would have to be funded externally either through government schemes or by voluntary action as had been the case in Wattstown a decade earlier. In the same council meeting, as if in anticipation of the council's new attitude, members of the Porth & District Public Baths Committee put forward their proposals for a swimming bath at Bronwydd Park to be funded by public appeals.[23]

For nearly two years, the local committee at Porth raised funds for a swimming bath until, in late-1935, the council decided to revise their earlier position and seek to provide three additional swimming baths across the district: at Porth, Ferndale, and in either Treorchy or Treherbert. The motion to locate the baths in

Treherbert was heard in December 1935 and relied on the votes of three Communist councillors to be carried.[24] RUDC's change of heart was encouraged by the designation of south Wales as a 'Special Area' under the Special Areas Act of 1934. Two commissioners were appointed to distribute money from a designated fund of £2,000,000. South Wales, as well as other hard-hit areas such as the North East of England, were provided with grants for public works projects that would not otherwise have been undertaken. Although often criticised for being ineffective and insufficiently financed, the impact of the Special Areas legislation on leisure in south Wales cannot be underestimated.

In total, thirteen swimming baths were constructed from funding distributed by the Special Areas Commissioners: Abercarn, Aberdare, Bargoed, Bridgend, Caerphilly, Cymmer, Edwardsville, Ferndale, Mountain Ash, Pantyscallog, Pontllanfraith, Porth and Treherbert. A fourteenth, at Maesycwmmer, received funding for its completion whilst those in Pontypridd, Abertillery and Brynmawr were all refurbished.[25]

The baths built in this period were immensely popular. During their opening weekend, for example, Gelligaled swimming baths were visited by 4,000 people. Half of those turned up on the first day.[26] That the vast majority were children (and continued to be

With the dramatic scenery of the Rhondda valleys stretching into the background, this photograph, taken shortly after the Treherbert swimming baths opened in 1937, shows the impact of new leisure facilities on the built fabric of the coalfield community.

children) delighted councillors who believed that the time of swimming in dirty rivers had finally come to an end.[27] Those who used the swimming baths recall, almost universally, the joyous times they spent there. W. John Owen, of Cilfynydd, remembered that the Cwm baths, a converted reservoir made safe and supervised by Pontypridd Urban District Council in the early 1920s, were a 'paradise for the kids and teenagers of the village'. Many hours were spent swimming and 'late-night barbeques with a sing-along were a great feature of those happy days'.[28] Similar enjoyment was had by the residents of Bala in the waters of Bala Lake where, by the late 1930s, the council had constructed bathing huts for the use of swimmers.[29]

By the outbreak of the Second World War, there were more swimming baths in more communities in Wales than ever before. The combination of government spending on public works to ease unemployment and a high level of voluntary action and mutual organisation prompted a golden age of provision for swimming in local communities. The construction of open-air and indoor swimming baths and children's paddling pools, and more makeshift designation of reservoirs, saw the number of local authorities operating facilities for swimming rise considerably: in the Rhondda of 1920, for example, there were no public baths. By 1939 there were four open-air baths operated by the council, a further bath operated by the local miners' welfare committee in Wattstown, and paddling pools at the major parks in Porth, Ystrad, Treorchy and Ferndale. In neighbouring valleys and in Cardiff and Newport, the experience was the same.

In north Wales, the impact of this golden age was more limited. Baths provision was concentrated in the coastal resorts and in the coalfields of Denbighshire and Flintshire. The combined effect of not benefitting from targeted welfare and unemployment schemes provided by central government and weaker levels of voluntary action, meant that local communities and local authorities across the central and northern counties largely failed to develop their provision for public swimming.

Long disappeared from the landscape, the open-air swimming baths in Morgan Jones Park were funded by a grant from the Special Areas Commission and opened in the late 1930s. This photograph, taken by Aerofilms in 1947, shows the baths in the shadow of Caerphilly's great castle.

Post-War: Going Indoors

The outbreak of war in 1939 brought to an end the remarkable period of growth in the number of swimming pools in Wales. For most of the late 1940s and 1950s, a swimming pool was far from the minds of local councillors and local residents. But, towards the end of the 1950s, with the announcement of the Empire Pool in Cardiff, attention turned to the question of providing new facilities, particularly indoor swimming pools that could be used all year round. A letter printed in the *Llantrisant Observer* in February 1957 summed up the prevailing mood: 'Please build an indoor swimming pool in the Llantrisant area. This is what residents of Beddau, Tynant, Talbot Green and Llantrisant asked when writing to the Clerk of Llantrisant and Llantwit Fardre Rural District Council'. The matter was discussed by councillors who argued that 'in view of the present circumstances, no action in this direction can be taken'.[30] By the time Llantrisant and Llantwit Fardre Rural District was merged with Pontypridd Urban District in 1974 to form Taff Ely Borough Council, two swimming pools had been built: the desired one in Llantrisant and one at Tonyrefail.[31]

It was the sheer cost of constructing swimming pools in a period of severe spending constraint that proved prohibitive for local authorities. Although many had drawn up plans to construct modern, indoor pools or to convert existing outdoor ones for year-round use, the only major swimming pool to be constructed in the 1940s and 1950s was the Empire Pool in Cardiff — itself the result of plans dating back to the late 1930s. Councillors, in the twilight of the inter-war years, had dreamed of a great sports village located on Wood Street in the centre of the city. The tired, 75-year-old Corporation Baths had seemingly run their course and were strikingly out of date for a modern city. With swimming competitions having to be hosted in the salt-water baths at Penarth or in the open waters of the Cold Knap lido in Barry because Cardiff lacked proper facilities for competitive meets, the local clubs and those with an interest in the tourist trade felt they were missing out.[32]

When Wales was awarded the 1958 British Empire & Commonwealth Games during the course of the 1954 games in Vancouver, the major difficulty remained the lack of an Olympic-size swimming pool in the city. Although Cardiff Council eventually committed themselves to building a pool at a projected cost of

£700,000, the project was nearly derailed by the financial insecurity of the mid-1950s and construction work did not begin until January 1956. It was very nearly too late. Behind the scenes, contingency planning had suggested the possibility of using the Cold Knap baths in Barry if no new pool was built in Cardiff itself but this was seen as an undesirable last resort. In the end, the baths exemplified the aspirations of Europe's youngest capital city and the restrained character of the 1950s. Designed by the city engineer and architect, the Empire Pool was strikingly simple — a semi-circular roof and plain brick façade that evoked the spirit of the Festival of Britain — yet, it was immediately recognisable and made an unique impression on the skyline.

Finally opened in April 1958, the Empire Pool was an immediate success. With temperatures soaring that April and May, many took to lounging in the sunshine in Cardiff's many parks and nearly 3,000 people tested the new waters on Wood Street. Most, much to the annoyance of adults, were children: 'the youngsters have the best of both worlds', complained one resident bitterly, 'I don't begrudge them their pleasure but it does seem hard on those of us who foot the not inconsiderable bill for the pool to be denied the use of it'. Those in charge of the Empire Pool believed that financial reality would eventually trump novelty and set about fixing the prices to encourage children to use Guildford Crescent instead. With tickets for the Empire Pool set at 1s and those for the Corporation Bath set at 6d, the Baths manager maintained that 'they'd trundle off […] eventually'.[33] Many children did make use of the old baths for swimming lessons but it was the Empire Pool that they most wanted to swim in.

The next major swimming pool to be constructed was the Afan Lido in Port Talbot. Officially opened by the Queen in 1965, the pool was originally an Olympic-sized swimming pool with a 10-metre diving platform and terraced seating for 950 people. One of the first leisure centres in Wales, it exemplified and typified the values of multi-purpose, all-in-one facilities that were to be built in large numbers in the 1970s and 1980s. The Olympic swimming pool was converted in the 1990s into an aqua-dome complete with slides and other waterpark features such as a wave machine, transforming it from a facility for rigid recreation into a child and family-friendly funhouse. These changes were the result of innovations at the original leisure centre in Swansea which was opened by the Queen in her Silver Jubilee year of 1977. With

The original, competitive purpose of the Empire Pool is readily apparent in this photograph taken by the Central Office of Information in 1962. The ample seating overlooks the Olympic-sized swimming pool and the dining gallery dominates the far wall along with the scoreboard (which is obscured by the Welsh flag).

slides and Wales' very first wave machine installed from the outset, the pool in Swansea marked the beginning of moves away from sport as the essential principle around which a swimming pool was designed, towards pleasure and more informal recreation. This mirrored changes in attitudes to parks driven primarily by ideas from the adventure playgrounds movement.

The growth of indoor swimming pools was also notable outside the south Wales conurbation. From the opening of Connah's Quay swimming pool in 1961, the movement gained significant momentum and reversed the long-standing trend of poor provision.[34] Some, such as Rhyl Sun Centre, which opened in June 1980, offered facilities similar to those in Swansea. Community swimming pools opened, for example, in Lampeter in May 1972, in Aberystwyth in November 1973 and in Cardigan in February 1977. Harlech swimming pool was also opened in the early 1970s. Ironically, it was claimed by the mid-1980s that Dyfed had 'too many' swimming pools and closures were planned across the county.[35]

Opened in 1958, the Empire Pool was the centrepiece of that year's British Empire and Commonwealth Games. This photograph, taken by Aerofilms in 1959, shows the iconic and immediately recognisable building amidst its surroundings with the Arms Park, Cardiff Central Station, the bus station and Hancock's Brewery (bottom left) all apparent.

A parallel series of changes in this period took place in those communities with inter-war open-air swimming baths. Recognising a clear decline in their use (mirrored with the rise in indoor pools), councils sought to find ways of converting as many as possible into simple indoor pools. At Maesteg, for example, the fine open-air baths that were built in 1938 at a cost of £8,000 were transformed in the late 1960s into the indoor pool that survives today. Opened in 1969, the conversion had cost £80,000

Rhyl Sun Centre, which opened in June 1980, was built at a cost of £4.5 million and was the first waterpark-style swimming pool in north Wales with wave machines, slides, a monorail and an indoor surfing pool (the first of its kind in Europe). This photograph, taken by the Central Office of Information in 1983, captures some of these new features along with a sense of their popularity.

and involved not only the construction of a roof and indoor changing rooms, but also the separation of the pool into a shallow children's pool and a deeper swimming pool for adults. Similar changes took place to the baths at Edwardsville in 1986 and at Porth and Treherbert in the early 1990s. For the most part, conversion has been the only way that open-air swimming baths dating from the 1920s and 1930s have survived in local communities. More often, swimming pools were part of major leisure centres built in the 1970s onwards, for example at Rhydycar in Merthyr Tydfil, at Pontypool, and more recently in the Rhondda.

The challenge facing open-air baths from indoor swimming pools and multi-purpose leisure centres since the 1960s has been immense and it is a battle that has been lost despite popular enthusiasm for the lidos. The lido in Abertillery was one such victim, having been constructed in 1900 by a forward-looking, progressive council it was superseded by a 1970s leisure centre and eventually filled in. Nothing now remains of the site. Not all baths were demolished quite so quietly. In the mid-1970s, for example, Cynon Valley District Council became embroiled in a fierce debate over the closure of the open-air swimming baths known locally as the Rock Baths. These had been provided in the 1930s by the Special Areas Commission and were regularly used by local school children for their swimming lessons and by Aberdare Swimming Club. Though the baths were to be replaced by a modern, indoor swimming pool, local residents were angered by the immediate demolition of the Rock Baths for use as a council car park. There were similar campaigns across Wales as local authorities closed down the remaining lidos throughout the 1980s, 1990s, and 2000s.

The loss of many open-air swimming baths since the 1970s has sparked several fierce local campaigns. This photograph was taken in May 1975 following the closure of the Rock Baths in Aberdare by Cynon Valley Borough Council and captures the anger expressed by many. The signs read: 'every time you park your cars stop and think of all the children you have done out of swimming in the sun' and 'enjoy parking where children should be swimming'.

Maesteg's swimming baths were opened in 1938 at a cost of £8,000 and later converted to indoor use in 1969–70. Unlike many of those built in the 1930s, the Maesteg swimming baths have survived and continue to be used today.

Legacies

Over the course of the first half of the twentieth century, in excess of fifty swimming baths were opened across Wales. From a germ of just a handful in the larger towns by the time of Queen Victoria's death in 1901, the rapid expansion of provision during the inter-war years had made safe swimming an accessible reality for a good proportion of the population. The facilities constructed by councils, by businesses and by voluntary action in the 1920s and 1930s formed the core of Welsh swimming provision until the combined effect of the leisure centre movement of the 1970s and the government spending cuts of the 1980s resulted in decline, dereliction and eventual demolition of the dedicated pool. From the loss of the first lidos in the 1960s (albeit often to conversion) to the closure of the 'last lido' at Brynamman in 2010, it has been a sad story.

It is now not an exaggeration to state that almost the entire network of swimming pools constructed in the 1920s and 1930s has been dismantled. Some such as those at Edwardsville and Gwaunfarren, that managed to survive the closures of the 1970s, have since disappeared. Both were closed in 2007 in exchange for state-of-the-art swimming facilities at Rhydycar in central Merthyr.

Another victim of closure in 2007 was Blaenavon swimming pool, which opened as a lido in 1921 and was roofed in the 1970s. Demolished during the Christmas period, a mock funeral was held by local residents in February 2008 bringing national attention to the plight of many community swimming facilities right across the United Kingdom. The *Daily Telegraph* reported in 2008 that Blaenavon was one of thirty pools that had closed across the country between 2006 and 2007.[36] Following that article, the converted pool at Treherbert lost its fight against closure in April 2009 and in Carmarthenshire, Hendy lido was shut in 2009 and Brynamman, known for much of the 2000s as Wales's last lido, closed in 2010.[37] The loss of older outdoor facilities for the sake of modern indoor leisure centres is, of course, not a recent phenomenon but the erosion of this particular aspect of the historic sporting environment of Wales has been especially pronounced.

Not all baths evoked a pastoral setting. Some took the neat lines of modernism to heart as this photograph of the open-air swimming baths in Garth, Maesteg, illustrates. In contrast to the swimming baths in Porth or Treherbert, this almost feels claustrophobic with the changing boxes lining both sides of the pool.

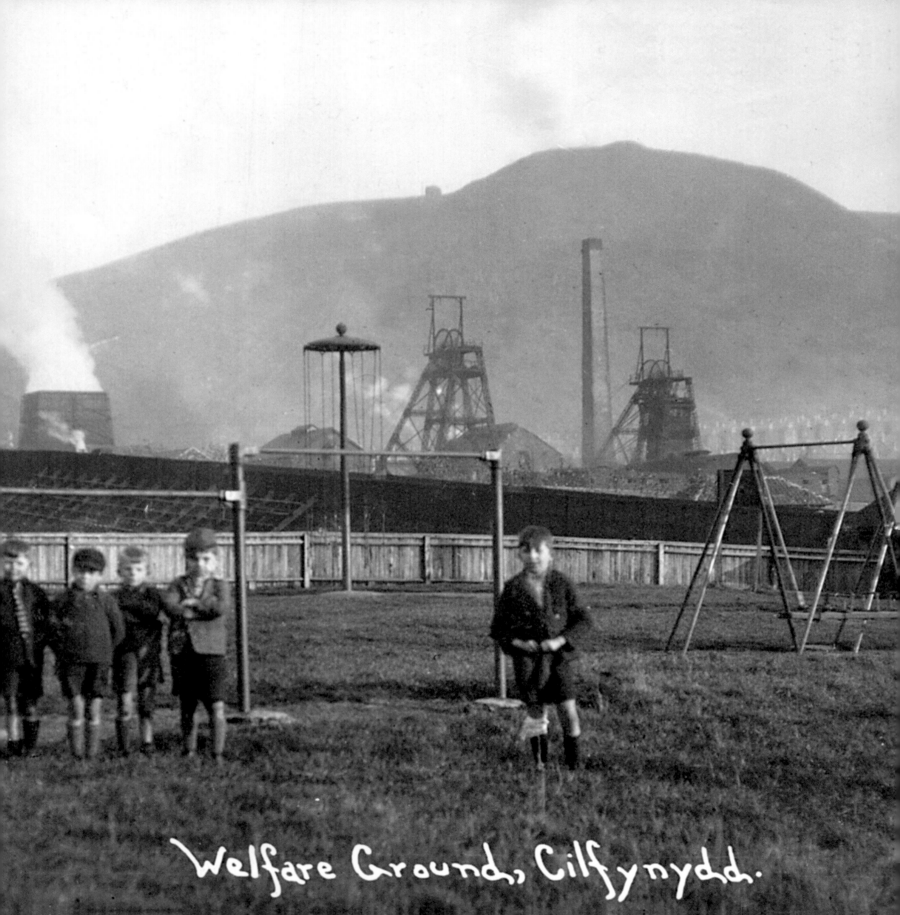

Welfare Ground, Cilfynydd.

CHAPTER III:

Welfare Grounds

If we don't like ourselves, we can alter ourselves only by altering this valley. How? That's the question I stumble over in the dark. That's the question I've been trying like the devil to get away from me in the last few weeks. I doubt if it will ever change. In the days of wealth and plenty there was life enough in this valley, raw, real howling life to change not only the valley but the entire universe.

Gwyn Thomas, *Sorrow for thy Sons* (1937)

For the most part, public parks and swimming baths are facilities provided for communities by benevolent others: aristocrats and business leaders exercising their philanthropic duty or local authorities carrying out the functions of government for the betterment of the people. During the inter-war economic crisis, this balance between the public and the private was challenged by a third way: voluntary action. Drawing inspiration from working-class mutual organisations such as the Co-operative, the Workmen's Hall and Institute, medical aid societies and the trades unions, the grassroots welfare associations of the 1920s and 1930s aimed at a transformation of the landscape of industrial Wales. They saw a future in which rich, green grass flourished in place of the stunted weeds that sprang through the spoil tips. The men and women who were active in local welfare associations in the 1920s and 1930s sought to remake the green valley for their own children.

The largest welfare movement was that associated with the coal mining industry which had formal, legislated mechanisms of funding and was in existence throughout the period. But miners were not alone in benefitting from changing attitudes to employees and, by the outbreak of the Second World War, most medium and large-sized companies, public corporations and

government agencies provided some form of welfare programme, whether in the form of recreational facilities, social clubs, libraries or something else. Bakers, railway workers, steel workers, police officers and miners all enjoyed improved access to sporting amenities as a result. What is different in the case of the miners' welfare grounds, however, is that these were open access and provided, typically by the voluntary labour of the miners themselves, for the betterment of the entire community rather than the discrete workforce of a factory or constabulary.

By the end of the 1930s, welfare schemes were responsible for providing public playing fields in many communities, particularly across the south Wales valleys where local authorities found themselves having to cut back their spending on amenities in order to meet the costs of alleviating unemployment while at the same time coping with falling revenues from the rates. Many of these grounds remain at the heart of their community even though almost all have been transferred to the local authority — a process which began in earnest in the 1940s when a combination of falling enthusiasm for outdoor schemes and financial pressures encouraged welfare committees to divest themselves of their playing fields in order to concentrate on the welfare halls and institutes. Yet, in spite of the circumstances in which they were built, these grounds encapsulated a remarkable vision and catered for a wide range of activities from rugby, cricket, soccer, bowling and tennis to croquet, crazy golf and quoits.

Welfare before the Great War

The origin of miners' welfare lies properly in the institutes and workmen's halls that once stood in every colliery village of the coalfield. Outdoor schemes — especially the provision of playing

Laid out on a small parcel of land opposite the Albion Colliery, Cilfynydd welfare ground provided a playing field and children's playground when it opened in the summer of 1925. The swings and other playing facilities have since been removed and the ground is used today exclusively for sport. The colliery closed in 1966 and became the site of Coedylan Comprehensive School (now called Pontypridd High School) in 1985.

Celtic welfare park in Garth, Maesteg, as it was in 1965. Opened by Vernon Hartshorn MP (Labour, Ogmore) on 24 May 1924, the park was provided for largely by the Miners' Welfare Fund and constructed by local volunteers. Aside from the cricket ground and bowling green shown here, the park included tennis courts and an open-air swimming baths.

fields and recreation grounds — began to develop in the 1880s and 1890s in communities such as Maerdy and Tredegar. Following the establishment of the South Wales Miners' Federation (SWMF) in 1898 and the emergence of the Labour Party as a viable political force across the coalfield in the first decade of the twentieth century, many mining communities turned their attention to the construction of workmen's halls and recreation grounds using a levy on miners' wages to fund their activities.

In 1901, the Lady Windsor Lodge in Ynysybwl was presented with a motion by Morgan Walters, a founder member of both the SWMF and of a local branch of the Independent Labour Party (ILP). Walters called on the lodge to approach landowners in the

village for a patch of land to provide a park.[1] Subsequent negotiations with the Plymouth Estate and Robert Thompson Crawshay came to nothing. Another attempt was made in 1906, but with the same result.[2] Frustrated at their lack of support from local landowners, the lodge committee turned to Mountain Ash Urban District Council for assistance and in 1910 was successful in securing an undulating piece of ground near the village school.[3] The council offered to fence it in, to pay the £30 annual rent and to maintain it, thereby transforming a workers' initiative into a municipal one.[4] Had the landlords been as willing to deal with the miners as they were with the district council it would certainly be recorded as an early example of a miners' welfare recreation ground. It had, after all, been the lodge that steered the community in favour of a park and organised public meetings to agitate for it.[5] Writing fifty years later, the secretary of the lodge, John E. Morgan, reflected that:

> Hundreds of children of both sexes [...] have grateful memories of countless delightful hours spent in its bushes and by-paths, playing 'Indians' etc., and many harassed and tired mothers also treasure memories of many enjoyable evenings in the sun upon its seats, where they had gone without dressing up, with their toddlers playing round on the grass nearby.[6]

This was miners' welfare (albeit moderated through council assistance) in its earliest form in a pit village that had been opened up only in the mid-1880s. Ynysybwl was not an isolated example: an early recreation ground had been laid out in Maerdy.

Institutes such as this were opened across the coalfields of Wales and provided for indoor recreation such as billiards and the cinema. They were also a focal point in the miners' welfare initiatives of the 1920s and 1930s. Mardy Hall opened in 1905 and cost £6,000. The original building was destroyed by fire in 1922 and a replacement opened in 1924. It was demolished in 2008.

It was, however, in Tredegar that early miners' welfare had its greatest success. The happenstance of a donation of land from Lord Tredegar to the workmen for a recreation ground to celebrate Queen Victoria's Diamond Jubilee in 1897 became something entirely more significant.[7] With annual rent and maintenance to pay as well as the costs of levelling the site and fencing it in, the working people of Tredegar took the fundamental step towards the miners' welfare model so evident in the 1920s and 1930s: they set up a ha'penny weekly levy which would sustain the recreation ground right up until the late 1920s when other, more commercial methods of raising maintenance funds including speedway and greyhound racing were adopted.

Few communities endeavoured to provide outdoor recreational facilities on their own before the Great War: the emphasis remained on the local authority and also on the private enterprise of sports clubs themselves. Nevertheless, this small number of initiatives demonstrates that the miners' welfare grounds of the 1920s did not simply develop as the result of government legislation but were already part of the wide-ranging vision that trades unionists and community activists had for their villages and towns. The formal legislation of the Mining Industry Act of 1920 provided the financial means to develop much older ideas and, when local people formed welfare associations in the 1920s, they did so armed with experiences of these earlier attempts to provide voluntarily recreational facilities of their own. Towards the end of his life, Abel Morgan — one of the leading activists from Ynysybwl — labelled the village a 'paradise' because of what working people there had achieved.[8]

For the Welfare of Society

During the four years leading up to the outbreak of the Great War in 1914, Britain was shaken by a series of large-scale, occasionally violent, strikes involving miners, railwaymen and dockers. In 1912, a largely successful national strike won the miners a minimum wage. They were determined to protect what they had won and sought to improve working conditions even further. Coalowner D.A. Thomas complained that, 'a dispute between labour and capital had become most acute in those districts where the Socialistic element had come to the front and was most influential'.[9] The Russian Revolution in 1917 heightened the tensions between labour and capital even further and strike activity was a continuing problem for the government.

With armistice in 1918 and a brief economic boom, the fraught industrial relations in the mining industry were calmed. But it was not to last. Strikes erupted across the country from the miners in Yorkshire to the policemen in London to the soldiers returning to a land not yet in keeping with Lloyd George's promise that it would be fit for heroes. With the threat of a national coal strike looming, Lloyd George's government announced a Royal Commission on the mining industry chaired by John Sankey to settle disputes and to decide whether or not to nationalise the industry permanently.

The hopes of many workers, and particularly the Miners' Federation of Great Britain (MFGB), were buoyed when the government reluctantly conceded that half the appointments to the Commission ought to be made by the Miners' Federation itself. Among the members were Sidney Webb, the president of the MFGB Robert Smillie and the economic historian R. H. Tawney. Sankey himself was to serve as Lord Chancellor in the Labour government of 1929-1931. In its interim report published in March 1919, the Commission hinted at its direction: wage increases of almost twenty per cent and a seven-hour working day. By the time the full report was published in June, nationalisation had also been added to the list of recommendations. Out-manoeuvred by Lloyd George, the miners felt that he had betrayed a promise made to accept the commission's recommendations. Instead of nationalisation, the coal industry returned to private hands in 1921.

One positive outcome of the Sankey Commission was the Mining Industry Act of 1920 which set up the Miners' Welfare Fund. This had, as its basic remit, the improvement of 'the social well-being, recreation, and conditions of living of workers in or about coal mines'.[10] It was widely believed that if miners enjoyed better standards of living and had opportunities to engage in hobbies other than attending lodge meetings and branch meetings of the Labour Party, then they would be much less prone to industrial action. The fund was comprised of a levy of 1d per ton of output based on the figures from the previous year and paid by the coal companies themselves. It operated at two levels: the Miners' Welfare Committee which oversaw the fund on a national scale and reported directly to the Board of Trade and the

Bedwellty Park and Tredegar Recreation Ground captured by Aerofilms in 1930. The speedway and greyhound racing track at the recreation ground opened the previous year with speeches given by the local MP Aneurin Bevan (he had been elected at the General Election of 1929). The more traditional parklands of Bedwellty were once the preserve of the town's ironmasters but became the home of Tredegar Urban District Council in 1900 and opened to the recreation of all.

twenty-five coalfield-wide welfare committees, which administered and distributed the Fund locally. Applications for assistance were made by welfare or recreation associations in the colliery villages and townships and therefore the facilities provided were very much designed and desired by the grassroots.

This multi-level form of governance ensured a variety in the type of schemes that were funded in each region. In Wales, the pattern broadly favoured recreational amenities such as the swimming baths at Buckley or the many recreation grounds and parks across the south Wales valleys. Figures for the South Wales Coalfield show that two-thirds of the revenue (in excess of £1.25 million) redistributed to the region was spent on facilities for leisure and recreation throughout the 1920s and 1930s.[11] This was not always popular, particularly with the coal owners themselves or those workers who felt that miners' welfare ought to be directed towards providing pithead facilities rather than outdoor extensions of the institute. 'The welfare of the miner at work', complained the *Ocean and National Magazine* in April 1929, 'is not yet considered as of supreme importance in our coalfield'.[12] The important contribution of the Miners' Welfare Fund to the development of pithead baths is remembered and celebrated. Its contribution in the forms of welfare grounds and open-air swimming pools, by contrast, has been largely neglected.

The number of projects that received funding and assistance across south Wales and Monmouthshire was truly remarkable: in just six years, 1922–28, nearly 120 separate recreation grounds

The breakthrough of women onto welfare committees took place in the 1930s. Elected as district and county councillors, women gained an increased presence in the political life of the valleys in that decade. With a singular vision, committees such as this one from Hirwaun set about providing parks, swimming pools and welfare halls that transformed their villages and towns in the midst of economic hardship.

were given financial support, and by the outbreak of the Second World War that had reached nearly 400.[13] In literally every coalfield community, there was a facility paid for, either fully or in part, by the Fund and success stories were reported regularly in the press and in national journals. This was the golden age of voluntary provision; with hard work, aspiration and utopian vision, those who were active on welfare committees or who laboured on levelling ground and laying out parks and playing fields transformed the landscape. Their rallying cry had been the pioneering Ministry of Health report on south Wales published in 1921 which remarked on the lack of land set aside for recreational facilities outside the seaboard towns such as Cardiff and Swansea.[14] They brought into being a more democratic form of sporting space than had previously been known and one which, in the plethora of sports included, catered for the leisure choices of the majority.

At the core of community action was the local welfare association. Set up fairly swiftly after the Miners' Welfare Fund was constituted in 1921, these organisations were generally offshoots of the miners' lodge or the miners' institute management committee and only in a handful of communities such as Caerphilly and the Graig in Pontypridd were they genuinely open to all members of the public. Dominated by trades unionists and Labour Party members, these were associations that held a progressive vision of a socialised society that worked for all. Many gave opportunities to unemployed, unskilled workers to lay out the parks and to disabled ex-servicemen who were employed as groundskeepers or attendants.[15] The welfare grounds were one of the great collective achievements of the inter-war years in Wales and without the efforts of the committee members and the volunteer labourers, the sporting environment would be much poorer.

Opened in 1926, the Ely Valley Miners' Welfare Ground provided much-needed recreational facilities, including playing fields and a bowling green, for the residents of Tonyrefail. This photograph shows the tennis courts along with the fine clubhouse.

The benefits of the fund were especially noted in more peripheral and isolated communities such as Blaengarw, Cilfynydd, Hirwaun, Nantymoel, Trehafod and Ynysybwl, where geographical distance from the centres of local government and local political power had led to neglect. In Cilfynydd, the welfare association was formed in the spring of 1924 and opened the first part of its recreation ground in a small field opposite the Albion Colliery the following year at a cost of £500. Developed over the course of the next decade, by the outbreak of war in 1939 there was a children's playground, rugby pitch and pavilion and putting greens. The chairman of Cilfynydd Miners' Welfare Association, Henry Holley, observed that the 'social progress of the district since the inauguration of the welfare scheme [has] been much more rapid that it had been before'.[16] The stimulation of community spirit and collective action was tangible.

By the middle part of the 1920s, miners' welfare grounds were being opened in increasing numbers. In some coalfield communities, such as Ammanford, ambitious committees developed networks of facilities that catered for satellite villages (in this case Tycroes and Saron).[17] Amenities were also becoming much grander with provision made for bandstands, gardens and other features more typically associated with Victorian and Edwardian public parks. This was stimulated, in part, by the model plans provided by miners' welfare advisers based in London. The recreation adviser, Commander B.T. Coote RN, believed strongly that 'no playground for lads will be of real value unless it is made so attractive that they cannot help appreciating the need to treat it properly'.[18] Perhaps the finest example of this was at the model playground in Ystradfechan Park, Treorchy but this was not an isolated case: Maesteg Welfare Park, which opened on 6 June 1925, included shrubberies, flowerbeds and a rose garden alongside its bowling greens, putting greens, tennis courts and children's playground.[19]

The success, or not, of outdoor miners' welfare projects depended heavily on a well-organised local committee, easy-to-work land and a good deal of voluntary labour. The latter was perhaps most significant since the tasks undertaken to provide a park in the hilly, rocky uplands of the valleys were Herculean. At Blaengwynfi, in the upper Afan valley, over 29,000 cubic feet of rock and soil was excavated from the site along Jersey Road by hand before the park could be laid out on level ground. In nearby Blaengarw, the local committee was told that the geography of that part of Wales made laying out a park extremely difficult. 'I can't help you here', explained one expert, 'you've just got to find the most level spot on this mountain slope and chop it out'. With a gift of £100 from the Ocean Coal Company to buy the best possible site, the labour began. Carving out a bank from the mountainside, dealing with drainage problems and landslides, the rugby pitch was eventually opened on 16 January 1927.[20] Elsewhere in the coalfield, the contribution of volunteers was made easier by the topography, even though thousands of hours were still expended on laying out facilities. In Llandybie, for example, volunteers gave the equivalent of 6,000 hours to develop a 4-acre site in the village that had been donated by the Earl of Cawdor to the welfare association and, in Nelson, the local unemployed spent similar amounts of time levelling and draining their own 6-acre site.[21]

The Wall Street Crash in October 1929 and the closure of many collieries across Wales in the 1930s placed heavy strains on the Miners' Welfare Fund and especially on local welfare associations which were reliant upon weekly contributions from employed men to continue operating. The South Wales and Monmouthshire Joint Committee spent much of the decade using its increasingly meagre resources to support schemes left devastated by colliery closures and ensuring that the gains of the 1920s were not lost forever. A special scheme providing thirteen weeks of direct payments was implemented with associations in Cilfynydd, Senghenydd and Penygraig all benefitting: the groundsmen were paid and the welfare facilities remained open.[22]

When this system of grants failed, local authorities were asked to step in and rescue grounds from being closed and lost. At Pencoed, near Bridgend, the Miners' Welfare Ground, which began with great hopes in 1925 and had expanded to 13 acres by 1927, was transferred to the local authority Penybont Rural District Council.[23] Similarly, the inability of the Senghenydd scheme to generate sufficient revenue even with the imposition of special measures meant that, at the end of March 1931, Caerphilly UDC was asked to take over the recreation ground there.[24] Such action proved to be vital in the struggle to maintain the successes of the 1920s. It was, however, a process that would prove to be very difficult to halt.

Laid out as a model playground, Ystradfechan Park in Treorchy was the showpiece ground of the Ocean Area Recreation Union (OARU), a combine of welfare committees linked by virtue of their collieries being owned by the Ocean and National Coal Company. It was here that the OARU had its headquarters and Ystradfechan was intended as an inspiration to local committees across the coalfield.

The Second World War brought the age of voluntary provision of sporting and recreational amenities largely to an end. The increased role of the state during the war and the fragile condition in which many welfare associations found themselves after the tumultuous years of the 1930s meant that the public park rather than the welfare ground prevailed. On the basis of the figures produced by the South Wales and Monmouthshire Joint Committee for Miners' Welfare, it seems unlikely that there would have been much of a revival in fortunes had the war not taken place. Miners' welfare was financially unsound even by 1939 and, by 1947, when nationalisation of the industry took place, miners' welfare grounds in south Wales alone needed a sum of

around £375,000 to renovate and improve them to the standards expected in post-war Britain. It was a sum far beyond the capacity of a district working with a budget, by 1945, of a little over £12,000 a year.[25]

A Most Interesting Experiment

The plight of south Wales in the late 1920s and early 1930s was recognised at an international level. Journalists seeking to understand the impact of industrial collapse and long-term unemployment travelled to the region soon to be designated by the coalition National Government as a 'special area'. In the summer of 1931, a group of international volunteers arrived in

Brynmawr to help to construct a recreation ground and swimming pool for the residents of one of Britain's most stricken towns. Not that this was immediately, or automatically, welcomed by all residents of Brynmawr, who feared the attention garnered by the international volunteers would overshadow the deep-rooted flaws of the economic system that had thrown so many of Brynmawr's workers out of work. As the clerk to the council put it in December 1932, 'no voluntary effort, however well-intentioned can solve Brynmawr's unemployment problem'.[26] It was a point accepted by all those who volunteered for miners' welfare projects. Building a swimming pool was something to do while there was no work but, if there came a choice between work and a park, a job came first.

Work in Brynmawr that summer was hard. The aim of transforming a rubbish dump into a swimming bath and gardens meant excavating and levelling rocky ground and having enough money left over to construct the pool itself. With many of the volunteers coming from professional backgrounds or from universities they often lacked groundwork skills and being taught by the local unemployed helped to bring the two groups together. For the women volunteers, their participation in the scheme involved getting up at half-past five in the morning to prepare breakfast before getting on with cleaning and washing and mending clothes, and often taking part in the navvy work themselves. For the men, physical labour began at 7 o'clock and continued on into the evening with time off permitted only on

Opened in 1932, the swimming baths in Brynmawr were built by voluntary action. Their simple, modern style reflected the aspirations of the town and its people amidst economic adversity. Note the tipi-style tents that some used to change in.

Saturday afternoons and on Sundays. Sleeping quarters were also basic: two empty rooms above a shop wherein straw mattresses were laid out. The women, who were housed separately, were eventually given beds to sleep on. The hard labour and simple conditions paid off; as one of the unemployed local volunteers put it: 'this is the best payday we've ever had'. The lido, which opened in the summer of 1932, threw into sharp relief that capacity of the community to help itself.

It almost didn't get finished. The project ground to a halt in early summer 1932 having run out of money before being in a position to purchase the cement to line the inside of the swimming pool. It was not until the timely intervention of the small village of Lagarde (today known as Albefeuille-Lagarde), which is situated in the *Midi-Pyrénées* region of southern France, that the problem was overcome. Inspired by reports of the efforts in Brynmawr printed in the French press, the Lagardois sent £153 to Brynmawr as a gesture of international solidarity and, in a letter accompanying the money, the mayor of the village offered the hope that peace initiatives such as the one at Brynmawr would replace war. When the baths opened in July 1932, the mayor was invited as guest of honour in order to reinforce the bonds of international friendship created by the project.

Volunteers from the International Voluntary Service returned to Brynmawr for one last work camp in 1938. One of the participants, Ernst Maier from Lucerne in Switzerland, wrote of his experiences during August of that year in his diary. 'The journey is long', he lamented, 'very long and tiring'. The trip from Switzerland brought Maier first to London where the grey skies and perpetual rain left him wondering 'is this England?' From there Maier took a train to Wales and eventually found himself on a little bus winding up and down the hills on its way to Brynmawr. The camp that summer was largely comprised of students from England and volunteers from Switzerland. Of the forty-two men present, two came from Germany, one from

---

With volunteers from a number of European countries as well as many of the local unemployed, the Brynmawr swimming baths were a unique experiment in international solidarity and peace activism. These three photographs, taken by the volunteers themselves and now kept at the International Voluntary Service archives in La Chaux-de-Fonds, Switzerland, illustrate the task that faced them in the summer of 1931.

Opening day at the baths! The importance of the **Brynmawr** project to the town is immediately clear from this photograph. Bonds of friendship developed during two summers of intensive labour had made real the internationalism for which the **South Wales Coalfield** had such a reputation.

Czechoslovakia, and one from Wales. The smaller cohort of fourteen women was slightly more diverse: five from England, four from Switzerland, two each from Wales and Scotland, and one from Sweden. They worked on levelling tips and waste ground and generally providing assistance on groundwork projects in the town, though none, it appears, was directly linked to the recreational amenities built earlier in the decade.

The 1938 camp was a muted finale to international voluntary effort in south Wales during the 1930s. Brynmawr had benefitted three times from the assistance of members of the International Voluntary Service (IVS) but the IVS held four camps in south Wales between 1931 and 1938. The fourth, which took place in the summer of 1934, was held in the nearby village of Forge Side on the outskirts of Blaenavon. The previous year, the local welfare committee had put into motion a scheme to provide, by voluntary labour, a much needed playing field for the community. With scant finances and occasional disagreements amongst the volunteers,

progress was slow. Being fully aware of the success of the Brynmawr project, the committee eventually elected to contact the IVS for their assistance.

A letter sent by the welfare committee in Forge Side to the IVS offices in Switzerland reflected not just on the paucity of playing fields in the local area but on the recreational practices of children living in Forge Side and Blaenavon at the time. 'The district is very badly off', the letter points out, 'so much so that the children wander into the old works, which are all open and quite near the houses, the old machinery being a great attract, numerous accidents are the result and, I am sorry to say, we have had a few fatal accidents'.[27] The 'old works', of course, now form a central part of the World Heritage Site at Blaenavon above which lie two rugby pitches laid out in more recent times. In interwar Blaenavon, however, there was the recreation ground situated at Middle Coedcae, which opened on 17 September 1921 on the initiative of the Workmen's Hall. Devoted primarily to

With Brynmawr spreading out into the distance this Aerofilms photograph, taken in 1932, shows the baths and the town together. They became a symbol of hope in a time of great hardship and news about the team of volunteers building the baths could be read in French, German, Swiss and Belgian newspapers.

organised sport such as rugby, football, cricket, and bowls it was perhaps less suited to the general games of children. Forge Side, by contrast, had no outdoor recreational facilities of its own until the mid-1930s.

Aided by financial support from the Special Areas Commission, international volunteers arrived in Forge Side on 17 July and remained until 22 September. An average of twelve men and three women were present throughout the summer (in total thirty-five members attended) mainly comprised of British, Swiss, French, and German volunteers. Though much less ambitious than the project undertaken at Brynmawr a few years earlier, the scheme displayed significant differences in its interactions with the local community. Volunteers were billeted with local residents instead of being separated from the people they worked alongside, thereby coming into closer contact with the everyday life of a depressed industrial community, and at weekends the IVS members were able to go on trips into the local area and explore different aspects of the towns and villages near Blaenavon.[28]

The Scheme in Forge Side was smaller than those at Brynmawr at the beginning of the decade. With international events soon to overtake the cause of peace, this cheerful salute was a happy end to nearly ten years of voluntary work.

The IVS did not restrict their activities to the towns of the South Wales Coalfield. The success of the Brynmawr camp in 1931 and plans to hold a second camp in the town the following year meant that the British organisations involved — particularly the Welsh Student Self-Help Council — engaged in a series of public talks to emphasise the good work done in Brynmawr, to attract new members and potential volunteers, and to publicise the potential of voluntary action as a means of responding to the ongoing

economic crisis. At one such talk, at Bangor in the autumn of 1931, Kitty Lewis was approached by a student from Rhosllanerchrugog who explained the difficulties that the village was experiencing in laying out a park at Ponciau Banks. Lewis saw immediately the potential to bring a group of IVS volunteers to north-east Wales and to expand the activities of the organisation in Britain.[29]

The *Wrexham Leader* brought news of the camp in its edition of 20 April 1932. 'In a few weeks' time', the paper reported, 'we are to witness at Rhos a novel experiment in community building very much on the lines followed at Brynmawr in South Wales'.[30] The camp began in early July with volunteers from the universities and from a broad range of nations including several eastern European countries and the United States. The 'American Section' consisted of around fifteen young men from Detroit and other depression-hit cities.[31] Amongst the students were a couple of gifted linguists who set about learning Welsh: a Lithuanian from Kovno University (now Kaunus University) and a Spaniard studying at Madrid University. 'If the Spanish Armada failed to conquer Britain', commented the *Rhos Herald*, 'one gay and laughing Spaniard has conquered the heart of Rhos'.[32]

Progress was slower at Rhos than at Brynmawr but more genial for the abandonment of the military-style regimen adopted in 1931. In an article printed in *Welsh Outlook* in September 1932, Kitty Lewis observed that 'they all have their meals at the Miners' Institute and are billeted with the unemployed', which certainly helped to fuse the two groups together. Perhaps most interestingly, the children's playground at Ponciau Banks was actually constructed by children themselves under the friendly direction of a Swiss watchmaker.[33] Two further camps were held in 1933 and 1935 and the three together are commemorated in a series of stone carvings that can still be seen at Ponciau Banks. The entire park at Rhos was not finally completed until after the Second World War but the three work camps organised by the International Voluntary Service are an important aspect of that park's legacy and one which deserves broader recognition.[34] In a radio broadcast that was subsequently printed in the *Cambrian News*, George M. Ll. Davies (who had served as a volunteer at Rhos and Brynmawr) reflected on the events of 1932:

I remember a whole village rising to this idea of making a pleasant place for its people. Rhosllanerchrugog is obviously in Wales. The name is not as bad as it sounds. It means 'the moor of the heathery place', but there is no heather there now, only the crooked streets and queer-shaped houses of an old mining village of 10,000 people. They are the most remarkable community that I know for independence, originality and enthusiasm. The miners' leaders were considering a plan for buying eighteen acres of desolate coal banks in the centre of the village and of converting them into gardens and bowling greens and football fields that the village had needed for twenty years.[35]

The transformative effects of the international and local voluntary efforts in Brynmawr and Rhos in the 1930s are today commemorated in the respective towns. Wrexham County Borough Council secured funding in 2009 to refurbish and restore Ponciau Banks and to install local history boards at the park to inform visitors of its origins. In Brynmawr, the local millennium committee of volunteers have rescued the fountain which lay at the heart of the lido and transferred it into the welfare park where it is now the centrepiece of a memorial garden. With an audio-visual display complete with historic photographs, the site restores the history of the international volunteers and their local comrades. Both parks, then, stand in fitting tribute not only to the willing work undertaken in Brynmawr and Rhos but, in a sympathetic way, to the voluntary schemes right across Wales that have long been remembered but rarely commemorated.

Miners in Rhosllanerchrugog took inspiration from the success of Brynmawr and transformed a patch of waste ground in the centre of the town into Ponciau Banks Park. This photograph, taken by Aerofilms in August 1970, shows the finished park with its Gorsedd Stones, bowling greens, and open space. Also apparent (towards the bottom of the picture) is the workmen's hall, locally known as the 'Stiwt.

Company Welfare

Miners were not the only workers to benefit from new attitudes to company welfare. Pioneered in the nineteenth century by Quakers such as the Cadbury family in Birmingham and the Rowntree family in York, company welfare developed a different understanding of the relationship between employer and employee at a time when attitudes to the role of the state as a provider of services were changing. Comprehensive schemes such as those provided by the Cadbury family at the Bournville model village with its better-quality company housing, open spaces and sports facilities became the basis for modern planned industrial communities across Britain, including the mining village of Oakdale in the Sirhowy valley. Companies provided recreational facilities, sponsored works teams and factory leagues, and generally enabled workers to participate in sporting activity. Or at least that was the aim. In practice, few companies were as enthusiastic as Boots the Chemist or the confectioners. In Gwynedd, for example, the only company-provided recreational spaces were at the aluminium works in Dolgarrog. The ramshackle playing field ostensibly designed to support the company football team was merely a layer of soil covering some old scrap metal and the swimming bath, which opened in 1913, had a disused railway carriage as its changing room.[36]

North Wales is something of an exception in having almost no facilities. In general, company welfare schemes came to be common in both the private and public sector by the inter-war years. Throughout Britain, companies recognised the attraction of sport and sought to utilise its power to reward their employees. For the workers themselves, the opportunity to play sport on guaranteed pitches with well-appointed facilities and in regular leagues was gratefully received. By the inter-war years, company welfare schemes were in evidence across the country, especially in towns and cities. In Wales, major companies such as David Morgan Ltd, Spillers Bakery, transport companies such as the Great Western Railway, and public sector corporations such as gasworks, tramways and the General Post Office all had sports and welfare associations of their own. These were often quite large: Cardiff Gas Company's athletic and social club, for example, had 700 members by the end of the 1920s and was vital in extending opportunities for working women to participate in team sports.[37]

Aside from the miners' welfare grounds, mining companies provided facilities for their own clerks and officials. The Ocean Coal Company sports grounds at Treorchy included bowling greens and a well-appointed, red-roofed pavilion. Describing the former as 'alluring and soothing', the company magazine saw these as evidence that the company had the welfare of its employees very much in mind.[38] In Cardiff, the Hayes Recreative Association — the social club for workers at David Morgan Ltd — had its ground at Mill Hill in Ely whilst the Cardiff Gas Company and Spillers Bakery both owned athletics fields in Grangetown.[39] Welfare institutes for the civil service, the Great Western Railway, and the Co-operative Wholesale Society (CWS) could be found in larger towns. Indeed, so common were sports grounds for companies by the 1930s that planning departments for local authorities often included space for them: 'I take it for granted that a works site of the size you mention would probably include a sports ground', wrote the clerk of Bridgend Urban District Council in 1929 in correspondence with a prospective new factory owner.[40]

Perhaps the most impressive of all company facilities built in this period, however, were the sports grounds for Lovell's Rexville sweet factory situated in Alderney Street in Newport. Featuring bowling green and pavilion, several tennis courts, and a playing field complete with its own grandstand, it served as the home of Lovell's Athletic Football Club for fifty years. Former players remember the ground as being of high quality compared with even the home grounds of professional Welsh sides: '[our] pitch was far superior to what Cardiff City or Swansea had', explains one ex-player, 'when those clubs come to us they say "Christ look at this dressing room"'. Others recall the origins of the ground: 'it was formerly a quarry; filled up with ash'.[41] Lovell's enjoyed the active patronage of the Lovell family in part because of an ambition to transform the soccer club into a major sporting outfit. With as many as four teams (including a women's side) being run at its peak, Lovell's Athletic resembled senior professional sides rather than a works team and the quality of the ground was a testament to that and a symbol that it had been achieved.[42]

In areas where land for sport was at a premium, company sides instead made use of public facilities. In post-war Aberdare, for example, the local railwaymen, bus drivers, and workers at the

This photograph, taken by Aerofilms in 1937, shows the extent of the recreational provision at Lovell's confectionery factory in Newport (to the left of the river). The fine soccer ground dominates. Also apparent is Shaftesbury Park with its playing fields and bowling green and the tennis courts associated with Newport Rowing Club further along the river.

Truvox factory all played their matches at the Ynys Fields whilst in nearby Mountain Ash, the members of Deep Duffryn Sports Club played their matches on the playing fields of Caedrawnant, Mountain Ash Urban District Council's new sports facility.[43] Even in Cardiff, where many companies provided their own grounds, for certain sports, such as baseball, public parks were the commonest location. Post Office sides, for example, played their matches at Llandaff Fields as did the bakers for the local Co-operative society whilst Merretts Bakery played at Roath Park.[44] Others, including the welfare club for workers at the South Wales Echo made use of the playing field beside the Cow and Snuffers Inn in Llandaff.[45]

For many public sector employees, including members of the police force, athletics represented an important means of maintaining physical fitness, building camaraderie and, for chief constables at least, ensuring that employees were not liable to waste their leisure time drinking or gambling their wages away on the football pools. Most constabularies in Wales were active in fostering sports teams for police officers. In smaller, poorer constabularies such as Merthyr, use was made of public facilities:

In an effort to keep policemen away from less becoming habits, constabularies actively promoted sport amongst their workforce. National police athletic competitions were organised and clubs also participated in local leagues. This photograph, taken in 1928, shows Radnorshire Constabulary Football Club at their home ground in Presteigne.

the Merthyr Police Athletics Club played its football, rugby and cricket at Penydarren Park and made regular use of the bowling greens at Thomastown Park.[46] Similarly, the Radnorshire Constabulary, with its headquarters in Presteigne, was able to use the local cricket ground near Stapleton House for team sport. Richer forces, often with aristocratic patronage, had private facilities of their own. Cardiff Police were gifted playing fields at Blackweir by the Marquess of Bute and by the end of the 1930s, the Swimming and Athletic Club had been given a playing field and dressing room (which was constructed in 1933) entirely for free.[47]

The emergence of a Welsh university sector in the 1880s contributed significantly to the expansion of this form of recreational welfare as the new university colleges sought to provide for the interests and desires of students and staff. From the outset, college principals were attentive to the need to provide sporting facilities but were equally aware of the limitations on land. At a meeting of the governing body of the University College of North Wales, Bangor, in 1885, the principal remarked on his fears for the physical well-being of the young men and women because of a lack of a recreation ground.[48] Students attending the University College of South Wales and Monmouthshire (UCSWM), founded in Cardiff in 1883, were quick to set up rugby and cricket clubs though they faced difficulties of their own in securing a field to play in.[49] Similar issues had faced the students at the University College of Wales, Aberystwyth, in the 1870s.[50]

Such was the significance of having recreational facilities for students that in the debate between Swansea and Cardiff as to which town should be the host of the UCSWM, arguments in favour of Swansea made much of that town's recreational possibilities. 'I unhesitatingly say', wrote *Briton* in the *Western Mail*, 'that Swansea is the best site for the proposed College because of the greater facilities it affords for recreation'.[51] Another correspondent concurred: 'it is far removed from the works, the smoke, and the densely inhabited parts of the borough, a fine cricket ground adjoins it, and a recreation ground lies further to the west. The steam trainway connects it in 25 minutes with the picturesque sea scenery of the Mumbles'.[52] The decision eventually settled in favour of Cardiff though the later development of significant recreational facilities around the college buildings in Cathays Park suggests that the points made in Swansea's appeals resonated with the college authorities.[53]

In Aberystwyth, the University College was renting fields in the town for sport from the early 1880s and purchased part of the Smithfield in 1887 for the use of the tennis club.[54] Until the Vicarage Field was acquired in 1908, through annual rent to David Davies of Llandinam, and eventually purchased in 1912, students regularly complained of the state of the facilities available. The university magazine hints at the poor quality of the rugby and soccer pitches in particular with phrases such as 'Smithfield again demanded a rest' common in its pages.[55] As E. L. Ellis recounts in his centenary history of Aberystwyth University, the Smithfield was known as 'Smithswamp' in disgust at its regular, unplayable state.[56] The Vicarage Field transformed the sporting facilities for the college and enabled the athletics clubs and university authorities to free themselves from strained public amenities. By the 1920s, the site had taken on many of its modern characteristics with the construction of the grandstand, pavilion, and tennis courts.[57]

A similar trend away from the use of public playing fields is evident in Cardiff. Student handbooks published in the last years of the nineteenth century indicate, as they do for Aberystwyth, the extent to which the student population had played a role in the over-extension of local authority grounds themselves. The college's rugby and cricket sides both played at the Cardiff Arms Park whilst the soccer side, which had no ground of their own, were forced to practice at Sophia Gardens and Roath Park. The two sports provided for on university land were tennis and hockey with courts at Colum Road and a hockey pitch to the rear of Aberdare Hall.[58] It appears that women's residences were the catalyst for provision of facilities for these kinds of sports since similar amenities to those located near Aberdare Hall were laid out at the University Hall in Bangor (opened in 1897). The local press describes what was available: 'the grounds [...] contain two large tennis courts, one ash and the other grass, and also a croquet green'.[59] No doubt the proximity of facilities for women's leisure was a necessary part of the gender segregation between male and female students that persisted throughout the Edwardian period.[60]

The growth in Cardiff's university playing fields began shortly after the Great War when the college was gifted four acres of land by James Pyke Thompson's estate on Llandaff Road, Canton – known as Cae Syr Dafydd – and the rugby and soccer clubs

The University College at Aberystwyth first acquired the Vicarage Fields in the early part of the twentieth century as a replacement for the boggy and difficult Smithfield. It features a fine late-Edwardian cricket pavilion and has been a mainstay of university sport in the town for over a century.

quickly moved there.[61] Although welcomed, these were soon insufficient to meet the needs of the inter-war student population and negotiations began in 1928 with the Bute Estate to acquire land for a rugby pitch. At first the college was granted use of a portion of land at Blackweir which was being shared between the Technical College, the Police, and Heathfield School. Though the land was obtained rent free, the college was responsible for all maintenance and could not put up a pavilion. It had use of the land only for a short time: the following October, the land manager of the Estate informed the registrar of the University

College that 'there was no possibility of the college having the use of any ground this winter'.[62] This prompted the purchase of 8½ acres of land in western Cardiff at Caerau which alleviated the pressure on Cae Syr Dafydd as the soccer, cricket, and hockey sides moved to the new grounds.[63] It was greeted with cheers by the Students' Association.[64]

Meeting the welfare needs of company employees and students was to be an important feature of post-war social democracy in Britain and it relied heavily on the willingness of companies and college authorities to spend money providing facilities and to continue to offer financial patronage. For the most part, this continued to be the case in the private sector until the large-scale privatisation of British industry in the 1980s and 1990s and a shift away from company welfare towards a more clearly defined split between an individual's working hours and their leisure time. A number of clubs — particularly rugby clubs such as BP Llandarcy RFC and Corus RFC (formerly the Steel Company of Wales RFC) — that began life as company teams in the early part of the century still carry proudly names that highlight their origins even though most have now become self-sufficient. A similar trend is evident in the grounds upon which these teams once played. The extensive leisure complex at Llandarcy is a useful example. Operated by BP until the closure of the oil refinery in 1999, the facilities were bought by private investors in 2001 and continue to operate as the Glamorgan Health and Racquets Club and the Llandarcy Academy of Sport.

Though they have since made way for a large car park, the grounds in front of the main university buildings in Cathays Park were once the home of tennis and hockey for students in Cardiff. This photograph, taken by Aerofilms in 1923, shows the extent of provision as well as the National Museum under construction.

Universities have fared significantly better. The rise in the number of students since the 1960s and the expansion of the university sector in the same period has encouraged the provision of bigger and better facilities. Combined with the emergence of sports science as a significant branch of study, university sports grounds have become leading venues in their own right. International matches have taken place at the University of Glamorgan playing fields in Upper Boat near Pontypridd, for example, and those at Swansea University now house the Olympic-sized Wales National Pool. Investment in these facilities continues to be seen as vital for the future development of university campuses and play a significant part in attracting students from elsewhere in the world to study in Wales. The more general decline in welfare provision for workers in the public sector has been, however, quite apparent over the last generation. Following the withdrawal of the state from operating utilities companies, transportation and heavy industry, the once thriving factory leagues have collapsed and the facilities sold off for housing or other development. Just a handful of clubs have survived including the South Wales Police RFC, which was created in the late-1960s, and Cardiff Bus RFC.

Nevertheless, despite the decline of company welfare schemes and the transfer of miners' welfare facilities to local authorities, their presence in the historic environment reminds us of different ways of providing amenities and that is extremely important. Without the many recreation grounds (not to mention the swimming pools encountered in chapter two) constructed by unemployed workers in the 1920s and 1930s, many valleys' communities would not have had a park of their own until long after the Second World War. Vision and a willingness to labour in the hardest of circumstances meant that small groups of people succeeded in transforming the world around them. They expanded the sporting environment beyond stadiums and public parks and gardens and provided true community facilities. Their legacy is second to none.

No modern university can do without ample provision for sport. Swansea University, nestled as along the striking coastline of Swansea Bay, is no exception. This photograph, taken by the Royal Commission's aerial reconnaissance in 2006, illustrates the ample playing fields and modern athletics facilities at Swansea as well as, in the distance, the King George V Field and the open space of Singleton Park in the foreground.

CHAPTER IV:

Sporting Places

If the place had been flat, it would not have been so bad, but time and again, in the deeper valleys, teams played on pitches with a slope of one in three, where they take their half-time slice of lemon in an oxygen tent, and have rubber barricades at the bottom of the ramp against which players and referee can be bounced back into play when they go hurtling down with their brakes burned out.

Gwyn Thomas, *A Hatful of Humours* (1965)

The advent of modern sport in the nineteenth century brought to the fore the need to set aside dedicated space in which to play soccer, rugby, cricket and the multitude of other games that today make up the sporting passions of a nation and its people. Throughout the landscape are rugby posts and cricket squares, bunkers, greens and tees, and everywhere a tennis court or two laid out in concrete or on pristine lawns. Many of these facilities were (and continue to be) encountered in public parks or in public recreation grounds but the sheer volume of sport being played and the self-sufficient aspirations of clubs meant that not all of it could be or would be contained within their boundaries. Private sporting places are thus a distinctive feature of sporting heritage and, though their history is closely linked to public amenities, tell a story of both direct involvement in the provision and use of sporting facilities by social elites and the sporting habits of emigrant groups such as Irish miners and Scottish estate workers. In their own way, sports ranging from bowling to golf and curling to hurling found their way into the landscape.

Not every sport, of course, has had a fixed imprint: boxing, which at various times over the last two hundred years or more can be seen as the pre-eminent sporting passion of the Welsh, often took place in pubs, in booths at carnivals, in the street or in other venues including stadiums and roller rinks.[1] Boxing, as the *Rhondda Leader* put it in 1897, 'is carried on in public places for the amusement of the crowd'.[2] Not all of it was considered to

be bad either. During the Great War, fights helped to raise funds for various relief committees across the coalfield. In 1920s Merthyr, the secretary of the Labour Club erected a marquee in its grounds so as to host boxing contests to bolster its finances and in 1930s Pontypridd, the Cottage Hospital benefitted from charity contests at Taff Vale Park featuring famous boxers such as Frank Moody.[3]

Fighters certainly trained in gymnasiums but these were rarely solely for that purpose and often located in pubs. Freddie Welsh, for example, prepared for his famous bout against Jim Driscoll

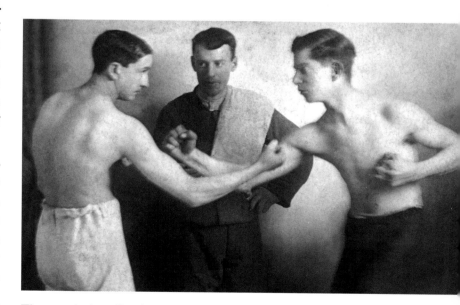

This photograph of a game of tennis being played amidst the ruins of the Bishop's Palace in St David's was taken by a Royal Commission investigator in 1934. Sport has often taken place in the most unusual of surroundings!

The popularity of boxing amongst the Welsh working class has been sustained for centuries. Fights have taken place on mountainsides, in carnival booths and in organised tournaments and professional bouts. In advance of contests, promoters often used posed photographs such as this one to advertise boxers.

This Aerofilms photograph taken in May 1933, shows Ninian Park being set up for Jack Petersen's fight against Heine Muller. Some 40,000 people gathered to watch. It was over almost as soon as it began with Petersen's powerful left and then right hook leaving Muller slumped on the ropes just two minutes into the first round.

at the American Roller Rink in Westgate Street, Cardiff, at a gym set up in the Clarence Hotel in Pontypridd. Driscoll himself could be regularly found in the upstairs gym at the Royal Oak on the Broadway in Cardiff. George Evans, a boxer from Merthyr, also knew of the intimate relationship between the pub and the boxing gym and noted that after the Second World War, 'many public houses closed their doors and with them went the boxing gyms […] Youngsters could only listen to old men talk about the old days when boxing thrived'.[4] A revival came in the 1950s and 1960s and new gyms were opened by boxers such as Eddie Thomas in many of the more deprived communities of the valleys providing opportunities and recreation for young men.[5] Enzo Calzaghe's Newbridge Boxing Club has continued this spirit in recent years.

The localised nature of boxing gyms typifies in many ways the relationship between sporting places and local communities. Smaller in scale, they offer active participation rather than passive spectacle. Whereas stadiums, which are the subject of chapter five, reflect the importance and commercial power of rugby, soccer and more recently cricket. Not all types of dedicated sporting spaces to have emerged in the last two centuries continue to thrive. Some, such as firing ranges, were laid out in the nineteenth century and provided for habits peculiar to their time and have subsequently disappeared. Others, including golf courses and commercial tennis clubs, have enjoyed widening success.

Holes and Greens

Golf is often considered to be one of Wales' youngest sports yet the first courses were laid out at the same time as the first soccer and rugby clubs were formed in the 1870s and 1880s. As with

The Glamorganshire Golf Club in Penarth as it appeared in 1929. Founded in 1890, this course benefitted from the patronage of the Earl of Plymouth who donated the land on the Penarth downs and met the costs of the pavilion, which opened on 13 July 1892. Initially a 9-hole course, it grew to a full 18 holes in 1896.

Opened in 1902, Radyr Golf Club is the oldest in Cardiff. This photograph, taken by Aerofilms in 1937, shows the clubhouse which was built shortly before the Great War. Notice the number of cars parked in the car park!

those rugby clubs which scramble to claim existence before the creation of the Welsh Rugby Union in 1881, the accolade of oldest golf course is a disputed one. Certainly, the earliest mentions of golf being played in Wales are at Tenby (in 1875) and at Ynyslas (in 1876) and, by the 1880s, 18-hole courses had been laid out at both locations. In common with cricket, golf benefitted significantly from the patronage and support of the landed gentry, aristocrats and middle-class professionals. Ynyslas, for example, relied heavily on the goodwill of the Gregson family until the mid-1940s and the Gwynfryn estate until the late-1970s.

Golf enjoyed significant presence in the coastal resorts of north and south Wales as well as in the suburbs of Cardiff where several courses were developed over the course of the 1890s and 1900s. The first of these was the 9-hole Lisvane Golf Club founded in 1898, followed by Radyr Golf Club in 1902, Llanishen Golf Club in 1905, and Whitchurch Golf Club in 1913. The course at Radyr was designed by the leading architect of his day, Harry Colt. Laid out on land originally owned by the Earl of Plymouth, it hosted the first professional golf tournament in Wales in 1904. Many of the original members of the club migrated from Lisvane since Radyr was easier to travel to. The Plymouth estate was an active sponsor of golf in the region having donated land to enable the formation of the Glamorganshire Golf Club of Penarth in 1890. Situated on the downs in lower Penarth, the course was initially a 9-hole course before being expanded to the full 18-hole in 1896. The Stableford Scoring System was trialled there in 1898.

In north Wales, the patronage of golf was even more impressive. Edward VII leant his support to Wales' first "royal" golf course, which opened in Harlech in 1894 (he did the same for Royal Porthcawl in 1909) and the sport soon spread to other resorts along the coast including Llandudno (1894), Prestatyn (1905), Bangor-St-Deinol (1906) and Caernarfon (1909). Deliberately designed to capture the beauty of their surroundings, courses in northern and southern resorts sought to throw off the windy-links stigma and to develop into tourist destinations in their own right. Courses in this region, including Wrexham, Pwllheli and Holyhead benefited from the design work of renowned architect James Braid whilst Abersoch golf course was laid out by Harry Vardon. These associations continue to attract tourists and budding golfers.

The development of golf summarises neatly the combination of tourism and the railway which fostered seaside resorts in the nineteenth and early twentieth century. Golf brought affluent visitors and until the widespread purchase of cars amongst the aristocracy, landed gentry and wealthier middle classes in the 1920s, the golf course was intimately tied to the railway network. Large hotels catering for the more exclusive tastes of golfers were established in resorts and hoteliers became shareholders of golf clubs. Suburban courses also relied on their efficient railway connections. The abandonment of the Lisvane Golf Course for that at Radyr was prompted by the better railway links to the latter. Similarly Llanishen Golf Club, which revived the abandoned Lisvane course in 1905 before moving to its own 18-hole course in 1923, would almost certainly have experienced the same fate had it not been for the Cefn Onn Railway Halt which served the course. Similarly, the clubhouse of Whitchurch golf club was originally situated near to the railway station in order to ease transportation. In all cases, membership of particular clubs confirmed an individual's societal rank in an age when such things mattered a great deal.

Laid out on the mountainside overlooking Ton Pentre, this golf course gained royal approval on 17 May 1924 when Prince Albert (the future King George VI) played a round during his tour of the south Wales valleys. The Prince lost the match.

The period after the Great War saw the emergence of workmen's courses. Mountain-top links such as those at Ton Pentre in the Rhondda formed part of the wave of welfare grounds that were built in the 1920s and 1930s. Largely built by unemployed workers in the early 1920s, Ton Pentre gained royal acclaim in May 1924 when Prince Albert (the future King George VI) played a round of golf with miners' leader and MP Frank Hodges. Short courses were also opened in public parks, usually under the guidance of Labour councillors, to provide a cheap place to play and by the 1930s councils were investing in golf courses of their own in an effort to extend opportunity. The course at Caerleon was amongst the first of these in Wales. Since the Second World War, the number of golf courses has increased significantly. In 2010, there were 200 courses at 185 different locations. The popularity of the sport in recent years has been allied to improved accessibility and affordability and the excitement surrounding the 2010 Ryder Cup. Hosted at the Celtic Manor Resort in Newport, this is the most high-profile golfing tournament to have been held in Wales and, despite the weather, was a commercial success.

Off to the Races

The dramatic rise of the number of golf courses in post-war Wales contrasts with the marked decline of horse racing as a major presence in the sporting landscape. Where once racecourses could be found across the nation in market towns such as Abergavenny, Brecon and Monmouth or in urban centres such as Cardiff, Swansea and Wrexham, today there are just three – Bangor-on-Dee, Chepstow and Ffos Las near Llanelli. Of these, Bangor-on-Dee, which held its first race in February 1859, is by far the oldest. Ffos Las, which opened 150 years later in 2009, is one of the youngest courses in Britain. Built on the site of an old open-cast coal mine, it was the first racecourse to open in Wales since Chepstow in the summer of 1926.

Racing has, however, been enjoyed since the eighteenth century. Recognisable courses were recorded at Cowbridge and Holywell in the 1780s and at Conwy, and Haverfordwest by the 1790s. By the early 1830s, these had been joined by Aberystwyth, Brecon, Carmarthen, Knighton, Tenby and Wrexham.[6] Going to the horses was especially popular amongst farmers and the gentry and these county town racecourses drew visitors from the surrounding

area. 'Nowhere is there greater enthusiasm evinced by the people', one racing newspaper observed, 'than in the land of unpronounceable names'.[7] Knighton racecourse, situated on the Newtown road, attracted patrons from Hereford and Shropshire as well as Radnorshire itself. In the north-east, the sport developed with the financial assistance and influence of major landowners such as Sir Watkin Williams-Wynn, fifth baronet. It was his involvement that enabled races to begin at Wrexham in 1807 and a switch of allegiance by his son, the sixth baronet, to the fledgling Bangor-on-Dee course in the late 1850s ensured the prosperity of that course. The first race run there was the Wynnstay Steeplechase.

In other parts of Wales, elite patronage was just as strong. In the first half of the nineteenth century, Brecon racecourse had been a relatively small facility drawing visitors and spectators from the surrounding area. Its fortunes changed in the mid-1860s when it attracted the financial assistance and influence of the Duke of Beaufort and Lord Tredegar. 'This little known Welsh meeting', wrote one racing newspaper, 'bids fair to take an important place amongst provincial gatherings'.[8] It was not to last and by 1868 the Brecon course's fortunes had turned sour. 'It is probable', lamented one supporter, 'that these favourite races have come to a dead stop'.[9] Under the influence of Lord Uxbridge, Lord Hereford and the Duke of Beaufort, Monmouth racecourse was substantially improved in the same period with an enlarged course and landscaped straights. Later in the century, Monmouth racecourse came under the patronage of Lord Raglan.

The fashion for horseracing also made its way to urban centres: in Swansea, for example, races were carried out on Crumlin Burrows as early as 1803 (when they first appear in the racing calendar) and were established as part of the refined entertainment on offer in that 'intelligent town'.[10] In the middle part of the nineteenth century, more modern racecourses were built replacing these earlier facilities. In Cardiff, the eighteenth-century Great Heath racecourse was exchanged for Ely Racecourse and, in Swansea, Crumlin Burrows was swapped for a venue in the Clyne Valley. With permanent grandstands and regulated access for ticketing purposes, these new racecourses ensured the commercial success of racing at a time of growing competition in the sporting world.

Chepstow racecourse as it was in 1929. Built by eighty men who transformed Piercefield Park over a period of three years, the racecourse opened in the summer of 1926 when, despite the intense industrial upheaval that had gripped much of Wales, 20,000 spectators turned up for the inaugural race meeting.

Most courses in the first half of the nineteenth-century were designed for flat-racing but the advent of National Hunt in the 1860s began to change all that. Manselton racecourse in Swansea, which opened in 1887, was a prominent example. The local newspaper described the new track as 'a right-handed one, of an elliptical formation [...] and scientifically constructed according to the rules of the Grand National Committee with privet quick and gorse banks, open, ditch and water jump'.[11] With a grandstand sufficient for 2,500 spectators and good access by rail, the course proved instantly popular. 'The sun shone for most of the day',

Ely racecourse on the outskirts of Cardiff opened in 1855 and enjoyed continuous use until it finally closed on 27 April 1939. Used for the Welsh Grand National from 1895, it was a prominent sporting venue in the town. This photograph, taken by Aerofilms in 1923, shows the racecourse near its peak with several large grandstands.

wrote one journalist of the opening races, 'and about 50,000 passed the turnstiles'.[12] By the early 1930s, National Hunt was far more popular than flat racing in Wales and the number of tracks varied accordingly. Flat racing was enjoyed only at the dual-purpose Chepstow racecourse whereas hunt racing could be found in Bangor-on-Dee, Ely racecourse in Cardiff, Caerleon and Tenby.[13] Yet, the closure of Tenby racecourse in 1937, Ely racecourse in 1939 and Caerleon racecourse in 1948 ensured that, in Wales at least, horse racing was a sport followed more in the bookies than at the track itself.

Caledonians and Hibernians

The emergence of the South Wales Coalfield as a major industrial region in the last quarter of the nineteenth century encouraged large numbers of migrants from across Europe to emigrate there. Although the influence of the English is well known amongst enthusiasts of rugby and soccer, the large numbers of Irish and Scottish migrants and their own indigenous sporting habits are often overlooked. Influential Scots such as Robert Forrest (the land agent of the St Fagan's Estate) and the Pettigrew Family (who worked as head gardeners for the Plymouths, Butes and Cardiff Corporation) were responsible for the import of the Scottish games of lawn bowls and curling. The bowling green at Sophia Gardens, which opened in June 1878, was ostensibly provided by the Bute Estate but in practice was the brainchild of the head gardener, Andrew Pettigrew. Designed for the sole use of Cardiff Bowling Club, the green was enjoyed largely by leading members of the workforce of Cardiff Castle. Though quickly emulated across the region, it began with very certain Scottish roots and enjoyed especial prominence amongst the members of émigré societies such as the Cardiff Caledonians.

Less famous and certainly less conspicuous in the landscape are the curling rinks built by Robert Forrest at St Fagan's and his close friend Macintosh of Macintosh at Cottrell House in the Vale of Glamorgan. Forrest was an enthusiast of the sport and was known to 'take a brush himself and sweep the ice clear, and then play very well'.[14] His curling pond, in the grounds of St Fagan's Castle, still survives hidden amongst the trees and was constructed in 1897. That at Cottrell House was built a few years earlier in around 1895. Typical teams included Robert and William Forrest, Andrew Pettigrew and the coal owner Archibald Hood for St Fagan's and Macintosh of Macintosh and the family piper for Cottrell House and reflected the high status of a number of emigrant Scots living in Wales in the late Victorian and Edwardian period.[15] Their influence almost certainly aided the spread of golf at around the same time.

Quoiting, which had significant following in industrial Wales before the Second World War but is now largely confined to rural counties such as Ceredigion and Powys, also benefitted from migration from outside particularly from Scotland and England. Though the game was known in Wales before the 1890s, it was in that decade that quoiting emerged as a popular pastime. In Merthyr Tydfil, Cwmaman, Cwmbach, Ystrad Rhondda and beyond, quoits pitches were laid out, leagues were formed and bets were taken on prominent players and clubs. International matches against England began in 1896 and against Scotland in 1931. For the most part this reflects the difference in pitch size between quoits as it was then played in England and Wales (an 18-yard pitch) and in Scotland (a 21-yard pitch). Ironically, the introduction of the 18-yard game to Wales in the 1890s seems to have come from a Scotsman and certainly interest in the game was fostered by émigré Scots and in Scottish newspapers.[16]

The sporting habits of the Irish are even less well known than those of the Scots despite a sizeable number having settled in Wales in the wake of the potato famine of the 1840s. For the most part, this is the result of their having being enthusiastic supports and players of sports generic to the rest of the population. Cricket, rugby, soccer and baseball were all fostered by the Catholic Church through organisations such as the Catholic Young Men's Society and these links produced long-standing sides including Dowlais St Illtyd's and St Peter's Rugby Club in Cardiff. Likewise, boxers, especially 'Peerless' Jim Driscoll, helped to forge strong associations between the Irish living in inner-city Cardiff, Newport or in the Valleys and the noble art. Consequently, the history of native Irish sports – especially hurling

Introduced by Scottish émigrés, curling was popular amongst a small section of Welsh society in the 1890s and early 1900s. This picture, taken at the rink in St Fagans at the beginning of the twentieth century shows a group of well-to-do men in the middle of a game.

Irish migrants also brought their own sporting pastimes with them to Wales. This photograph, taken of a hockey game in Carmarthen in about 1900, gives a sense of what hurling – then played with similar equipment – would have looked like.

and Gaelic football – and their presence in Wales has been generally forgotten.

It was not until a few years before the Great War that a younger generation of Irish migrants, whose sporting habits had been shaped by the Gaelic Athletic Association (GAA) since its foundation in 1884, began to form clubs dedicated to their own games. In other cities where the Irish diaspora was sizeable, including Liverpool, London, Manchester, Birmingham and Glasgow, GAA clubs were set up as a means of maintaining greater links with home. Soccer and rugby clubs that celebrated Irishness such as the Cardiff Celtics or Newport Hibernians certainly existed but when tours of Waterford or Cork by these teams took place, they were typically framed more by 'home-coming' rather than by nationalist fervour.[17]

The hurling clubs of founded in south Wales between 1912 and 1923 were rather different. At a meeting of the Irish community living in Splott in 1923, it was resolved to 'assist in every way the diffusion of the native drama, sports and pastimes' and the sentiment resounded throughout the region.[18] By then it was perhaps a bit too late. Nevertheless the existence, over the course of the previous decade, of hurling sides in Bargoed, Cardiff,

Maesteg, Merthyr Tydfil, Mountain Ash, Neath, Pontypridd, Swansea, Tonypandy and Treorchy highlighted a fairly widespread enthusiasm not only for the overt nationalism associated with the GAA – these clubs were given names evoking Irish rebel leaders such as, Patrick Sarsfield, Robert Emmet and General Wolfe Tone – but also the enjoyment of playing games other than rugby and soccer. Surprisingly, perhaps, hurling was played on pitches that were often right at the heart of communities: in Merthyr Tydfil, the local side made use of the Rhydycar playing field (the site of today's leisure centre) and in Pontypridd they played on Ynysangharad Fields (today's park).[19] In Cardiff, meanwhile, matches took place in the Arms Park, at Sophia Gardens and in Llandaff Fields and in Maesteg, a field adjacent to the town cemetery is still known as the hurling field.

The impact of hurling on the landscape was minimal but its presence in the sporting culture of Wales in the first quarter of the twentieth century highlights the richness and complexity of Welsh society. On August Bank Holiday, 1913, thousands of people flocked to the Arms Park to watch a hurling match and many thousand more read about it in the newspapers in the days that followed despite the sport having relatively little presence in

This photograph, taken by Aerofilms in 1932, captures a once common sight in the south Wales valleys: a handball court. Besides the famous court at Nelson, few have survived. This one, at Pontypridd Boys' Grammar School (later Coedylan Comprehensive School) has sadly fallen into the bushes and trees behind.

popular consciousness. Little more than a decade later, hurling had ceased to be played in an organised way in Wales and it was not until after the Second World War and renewed Irish migration that the sport was picked up again. Irish sport, today, is almost exclusively played in Cardiff.

Handball, which is traditionally associated with the Irish particularly in the origins of the court at Nelson, is in actual fact a much older game that has been played in Wales since pre-industrial times. Then known as fives, the game was played in villages such as Ynysybwl and Mountain Ash and later in schools such as Lewis in Pengam and Pontypridd Grammar. Irish migrants certainly played the game alongside native handball enthusiasts and this no doubt

helped in their own transition to life in industrial Wales. Few courts have survived intact today. The outlines of courts can be found at Jersey Marine and in Llantrisant but it is the fine court in Nelson, where international matches are still played, that stands as a reminder of this once popular folk sport.

Sporting Places

Specialised facilities came to be constructed for a variety of less prominent sports in the 1890s and 1900s in part because of a degree of reluctance shown by several local authorities to provide fixed locations within public parks. A general belief amongst councillors that their new and often quite expensive facilities should be for all and not the few stood in opposition to the genuine need for playing fields to support the growing numbers of teams across a widening number of activities. Rugby and soccer and cricket were generally exempt from this posturing, whereas hockey clubs in Cardiff, for example, were given short shrift by the Chairman of the Parks Committee, Ebenezer Beavan, when they asked to hire a part of Llandaff Fields for an entire season. 'We cannot do that', replied Beavan, 'We cannot set aside patches of land for these clubs. The ground is the ratepayers' and is open to all the ratepayers to make use of'.[20] Though the council later relented and hockey was played at Llandaff Fields by the two major Cardiff clubs — Cardiff and Cardiff West —, for the most part hockey clubs sought refuge in private grounds until the inter-war years when parks and recreation grounds came to dominate. This reality was promoted in several quarters. In the view of the *Western Mail*: 'in a private field [...] the committee can have a free hand in making a good ground'.[21]

Private facilities were also the mainstay of tennis and to a large extent this remains true in the twenty first century. Private lawn tennis clubs such as those in Penarth, Roath, Wrexham and Denbigh became extremely fashionable places to be seen. Tennis tournaments that drew competitors from across Wales were held as society events and the sport provided for the recreation of both men and women. In common with cricket, bowls and golf, the tennis club was as much defined by its pavilion as by the quality of its courts. This was especially true of the Queen's Road tennis courts in Aberystwyth, which opened in the 1930s. Showing similarities with other buildings constructed in the town in the same period including the clubhouse at Aberystwyth golf course, it spread over two storeys and was built in an attractive mock

By the time this photograph of Briton Ferry Hockey Team was taken at Jersey Park in 1924, hockey was widely played across Wales. Long-standing international fixtures against Ireland had been in place since the 1880s and many miners' welfare ground and public parks provided hockey pitches for teams to play on.

Pavilions, like players, came in all shapes and sizes but few were quite like this one at Presteigne. Nestled on the English border, this nineteenth-century cricket pavilion was built in timber with a thatched roof.

Tudor style and provided live-in accommodation for the groundsman as well as changing rooms for men and women and a function room. A large verandah at the front of the building faced onto the courts. These courts were operated by the local council as part of its provision for tourists but many tennis clubs before the Great War developed through the patronage of private benefactors including the Earls of Plymouth, the Marquesses of Bute and the Tredegar family.

Whilst tennis, bowls, rowing and hockey survived and thrived in the twentieth century, other sporting habits picked up in the nineteenth century have fared less well. This is especially true of the two principal martial sports of the period, archery and rifle shooting. The latter was fostered especially by the creation, in 1859, of the Volunteer Force. An early form of Home Guard, the Volunteers were ostensibly formed to bolster home defence at a time when a large proportion of the British standing army was stationed overseas — particularly in India — and reflected the sense of patriotic duty that was rising amongst the middle class. In the words of the *North Wales Chronicle*, 'All history shows that a nation is in a miserable position when it loses its military values'.[22] By the early part of the 1860s, companies had been formed in every county with large numbers of working men on the rolls. Though this was perhaps unexpected given the large costs involved in being a member of a rifle company – purchasing suits cost on average £4 10s and the government provided only a certain proportion of guns and ammunition – many wealthier patrons subscribed significant amounts in order to ensure equal access for all sections of society. One gentleman in Rhyl, for example, offered £50 if a corps of 100

The rifle range emerged as a sporting venue in the mid-nineteenth century and remained in use, albeit intermittently, until the end of the Great War. These photographs taken at Merthyr Mawr near Bridgend in 1931 show the abandoned rifle butts and shooting gallery. The gallery still survives poking out of the sand dunes.

Though the rifle companies were formed for defence purposes, they quickly became an avenue for recreation with shooting competitions regularly held at the many rifle ranges that were built in the nineteenth century and at volunteer sports that were taking place in the summer months. In addition to shooting butts and target galleries, companies also constructed drill halls many of which survived long into the twentieth century as public venues. The opening of one in the north Wales mining village of Gresford was welcomed as providing 'a place in which its people can congregate during the months when Nature withdraws her charms'.[25] Paid for by the landlord of the Plough Hotel, George Aingworth, it is a single-storey brick building and has survived as a youth centre. In nearby Denbigh, the large drill hall situated on Love Lane was built in 1882 and was flanked by the drill instructor's house and an educational centre. Today, it is used as a snooker hall. Architecturally, the Drill Hall in Denbigh is strikingly similar to that which still stands in Poyser Street in Wrexham and was built in 1902. In Swansea, which claimed the largest drill hall in Wales at the time of opening in June 1883, the ambitious offerings were matched in the Tuscan styling of the building. Constructed at a cost of £4,000 on the site of a former malt house, there was both a large and lesser hall providing for public entertainment including concerts and dancing as well as military drill and practice. It was demolished in 1897 to make way for the Grand Theatre.

In a similar fashion, archery emerged in the nineteenth century as a sporting practice rather than a military one. At first, it developed around the social habits of aristocrats whose romantic imaginations were fuelled by a love of the gothic and medieval. Hosting archery tournaments in the grounds of old castles such as Cardiff and Raglan or in the lavish gardens of country estates such as Nanteos near Aberystwyth, Aberglasney in Carmarthenshire or Speech House in the Forest of Dean offered a link, however tenuous, to the imagined pleasures of the past. As with the costumes bought by rifle volunteers, companies of bowmen also dressed in distinctive uniforms although this passed out of fashion in later decades as archery became popular with the more rational and self-improving middle class. Unusually for the period, archery thrived as a sport as much for woman as men and though the sport sought to entrench rather than challenge traditional attitudes to femininity, it provided crucial opportunities for women to enjoy sport and recreation of their own. By the

men could be formed there.[23] As a result, the popularity of rifle shooting in the 1860s and 1870s was fairly widespread and more socially inclusive than might be first imagined. 'There has been a very general complaint throughout the country that nearly every Volunteer Rifle Corps that has been established partakes too much of the upper and middle class element', observed one Wrexham commentator in 1860, '[but] there are now as many working men in the corps as there are middle class or professionals'.[24]

Edwardian period, these associations and the rejection of Victorian medievalism prompted a decline in the popularity of archery as a sport and facilities were either left to decline or replaced with more fashionable games including tennis and hockey.

Passing fashions yielded a number of more unusual activities in the latter part of the nineteenth century and into the twentieth. Roller skating, which enjoyed popular success in the coastal resorts of north Wales in the 1870s and in Cardiff in the 1890s, was one such fad. Imported from America, roller skating and roller hockey were promoted as healthy, fulfilling exercise and which further developed skating skills learned on the ice during the winter. 'There is grace in the movements of a skilful skater' opined the *North Wales Chronicle* in 1875.[26] The skating rinks opened in

Llandudno and Rhyl were owned and operated by the Roller Skating Company Limited based in Middlesbrough and offered day and night entertainment through the judicious use of gas lamps to impress patrons with a spectacle of light and colour in the evenings. 'Society', the local press concluded, 'may now be said to be upon wheels'. By the end of the 1870s, rinks had also opened in Bangor and in Adamsdown in central Cardiff and a temporary rink had also been provided in the Denbigh Assembly Room.[27]

The opening of Stoll's Panopticon at the Philharmonic Hall in Cardiff in April 1893 returned roller skating to the Welsh metropolis in lavish fashion. Its success was immediate and within a week of opening the *Western Mail* found that it had 'caught on immensely'.[28] Over the course of the next twenty years, skating

A large corrugated iron structure situated on Westgate Street in central Cardiff, the American Roller Rink opened in 1908. This photograph, taken in advance of Jim Driscoll's bout with Freddie Welsh on 20 December 1910, shows the rink being used for sporting purposes. The rink was dismantled in 1919 and moved elsewhere in the city.

rinks were opened in communities across Wales including the American Roller Rink on Westgate Street, Cardiff, which opened in 1908. Used for numerous sporting events and political rallies, it was here that Jim Driscoll fought Freddie Welsh in front of 10,000 people in 1910. Early in the same year, perhaps the most infamous roller rink in Wales was opened in Tonypandy. Here, during the riots that November, officers of the Metropolitan Police were billeted as part of the official response to the disturbances. In all rinks, patrons enjoyed roller skating as both sport and general recreation with many young people learning to dance on wheels. Roller rinks have now gone entirely out of fashion and have survived only in seaside resorts such as Barry and at the Urdd camp in Llangranog. In-line roller hockey has survived as a minority sport in Swansea, Cardiff, Carmarthen and Caerphilly with matches taking place in local leisure centres in organised leagues.

Many of these less popular sports have found homes in unlikely places and often they were played in grounds long associated with other activities. This is particularly true of the Arms Park. Though it has its own story as a stadium for international and top-flight club rugby the playing fields there have been nevertheless a central place for sports such as lacrosse that have not found a permanent home of their own.

Across Wales, then, places and spaces that provide opportunities and variety ahead of commercial profits have made a significant impact on the landscape and heritage of sport particularly at the local level. Whilst stadiums remain, instinctively, the main focus of contemporary sporting activity it is the private grounds, gymnasiums and golf courses that offer those forms of recreation that are not possible in public parks and in recreation and welfare grounds. In common with these, the facilities are often designed around the players and officials rather than paying customers and involve members in the decision-making process. In that sense, these sporting places represent a mid-way between the public and the commercial and link the two quite different forms of heritage together.

One of the more unusual sports to have been played at the Arms Park is lacrosse, shown here in about 1910. With its origins in North America, lacrosse was featured at the 1904 Olympics in St Louis, Missouri, and at the 1908 Olympics in London when Canada defeated Great Britain to win the gold medal.

CHAPTER V:

Stadiums

The Arms Park is the great shrine. The memories of the great games that have been played there have been worn as smooth as pebbles by every talking group in the taverns and clubs of the region.

Gwyn Thomas, *A Welsh Eye*, 1964

In twenty-first century Cardiff, one building dominates the city centre more than any other: the Millennium Stadium. From right across the city, its distinctive form and metalwork can be seen before other landmarks such as Cardiff Castle, the University and City Hall. Just as cathedrals and castles and parliaments and palaces lie at the heart of the ancient capitals of Europe, so the youngest of them celebrates its status (and that of its nation) not in the great buildings of the past but in a truly modern one. It was not always this way. Before the development of the Arms Park into *the* major arena for Welsh rugby football in the mid-1930s, the immediate impact of sport on the city's skyline was relatively slight. In those years, the Welsh metropolis was more typical of its nineteenth-century cousins with the Edwardian Baroque largesse of City Hall and the reconstructed fantasy of Cardiff Castle having a greater presence.

The emergence of the Arms Park as Cardiff's iconic structure began in the 1880s with the erection of the ground's first stand. Though a relatively simple building, it was part of a wave of development right across Britain and Ireland that transformed sport into one of the major commercial industries in the world. At all levels, clubs benefitted from the patronage of sympathetic landowners, farmers or councillors in gaining fields to use as home grounds. Often, these were slowly developed into enclosed arenas with a covered grandstand. For a select number of fortunate clubs, however, the support of wealthy industrialists and aristocrats enabled not only the enclosure of grounds but also the

construction of pavilions, terraces and other features typical of stadiums in large towns and cities.

Together, these facilities shielded large sections of the ground from the gaze of those who had not paid their entry fee and encouraged a mixture of patrons. Covered grandstands provided shelter and more comfortable accommodation for higher-paying customers, and pavilions, sometimes grand but often simply arts and crafts, offered committee rooms, the earliest equivalent of a corporate box and gymnasiums for players to train in. With each success and greater financial clout, clubs were able to transform their grounds, bit by bit, in order to provide greater spectacle for customers and to ensure that it was available only to those men and boys (and less often women and girls) who held a ticket.

Origins

The emergence of dedicated spaces for sport in Wales, as is the case in much of England, is linked to the growth of cricket in the first half of the nineteenth century. Clubs organised themselves into leagues and the regularity of competition meant that playing fields had to be secured for the entire season. Benefitting from the patronage of local landowners and the enthusiasm of publicans, cricket grounds were laid out either near public houses or on the estates of the landed gentry and aristocratic families who first took up the game alongside the professional middle class. The home ground of Raglan Cricket Club, which was founded in 1824, was a field behind the Beaufort Arms; in Montgomery, the cricket club were given the use of Lymore Park by the Herbert Family in the 1840s; and in Cardiff, the Marquess of Bute's offer to a floundering cricket club to make use of the river meadow at the back of the Cardiff Arms in 1848, not only helped to reverse the fortunes of that club but also laid the foundations of Wales's most significant and historic sporting arena: Cardiff Arms Park.

Nestled along the banks of the River Taff, the Arms Park established itself as the premier sporting venue in Wales. By the time this photograph was taken in 1932, the ground was being regularly used for international rugby union, county cricket and greyhound racing. Spot the number of cars parked behind the cricket pavilion!

With the cricket season over, the playing fields of Monmouth Cricket Club have been taken over by circus tents. The club first used the ground in 1842.

Many of the grounds set aside for cricket in those Victorian summers remain core elements in the wider sporting landscape of communities today. In Neath, for example, the Gnoll began in the late 1840s as a cricket ground before developing facilities for rugby in the 1890s. Likewise, Farrar Road in Bangor, the home ground of Bangor City until December 2011, was first recognised for its sporting potential not by the soccer club who played their home matches in the Hirael district of the city but by the cricket club. Only after the Great War, with their ground converted into allotments, did Bangor City move to Farrar Road. In Pontypridd, too, the establishment of Ynysangharad Park as a leading sporting venue in the 1920s – it hosted the first county cricket match in Wales to be played outside Cardiff or Swansea – owed much to the ground having been the home of Pontypridd Cricket Club since the 1870s.

The Gnoll, Neath, as it appeared in 1959. Famous as a rugby ground since the late-nineteenth century, the Gnoll has an even older cricketing history. Many players enjoyed rugby in the winter and cricket in the summer and several grounds similarly doubled up. Those who could not kick or bat a ball in Victoria Gardens found refuge here.

Soccer by the Sea in Holyhead! Now the site of the ferry terminal for passengers travelling to and from Dublin, until the 1960s it was a soccer ground. With superb views out into the Irish Sea and with the hustle and bustle of an important port across the harbour, it would have been a unique playing experience.

By the last quarter of the nineteenth century, the sporting passions of the majority of the Welsh had switched to rugby and soccer and grounds began to develop independently of cricket. In Holyhead, for example, the major soccer ground was laid out and used exclusively for that purpose and had no association with the summer game. Situated overlooking the inner harbour and with views out into the Irish Sea, the playing field at Turkey Shore was perhaps the most striking in north-west Wales. In the south, the

Penydarren Park in Merthyr Tydfil as it was in 1959. Situated on a hill overlooking the town, the site was once used by the Romans for their local military encampment and during the industrial revolution became part of the Penydarren House estate. Open to locals for walking, athletics and cycling in the late-nineteenth century, it was transformed in the first part of the twentieth century into a venue for professional sport: initially rugby league and subsequently soccer and greyhound racing.

picture was made more complex by the emergence of 'people's parks' and commercial recreation grounds: these were in effect multi-sport venues. The former, such as the People's Park in Pontypridd, were essentially carnival grounds but also offered playing fields for sports clubs. Typically, the facilities were larger and offered a number of sports such as bowling, tennis, cycling, cricket and rugby or soccer on one site.

Penydarren Park in Merthyr Tydfil and St Helen's in Swansea were amongst the most prominent examples of multi-use sports grounds. St Helen's and the adjacent Swansea Bay Recreation Ground provided facilities for rugby, cricket, soccer and cycling and was in use from the mid-nineteenth century onwards. Penydarren Park, similarly, came to be used for multiple sports. In use as an athletics and team-sports venue for much of the century, it was redeveloped in the 1890s with a cinder running track and cycling track to cater for the boom in foot and cycle racing that took place in that decade. Only with the formation of Merthyr Tydfil Football Club in 1909 did it become exclusively a soccer ground. Similar development of the Vetch field at the end of the 1890s saw the construction of a cycling track there. This was demolished prior to the establishment of Swansea Town in 1912.

The success of recreation grounds such as these encouraged entrepreneurs to set up multi-purpose sites of their own. The Harlequins ground, situated on Newport Road in Cardiff, was an early example of this type of commercial endeavour but it was the consortium which operated Alexandra Park in Canton and the separate consortium which operated Taff Vale Park in Pontypridd that took the business model to its logical conclusion. Laid out over 22 acres of prime development land adjacent to the Steam Flour Mills in Canton, Alexandra Park was opened in March 1880.[1] Its design provided for horse racing, trotting and cycling on specialist tracks as well as playing facilities for cricket, rugby and soccer. A well-appointed grandstand provided seating accommodation for spectators as well as committee rooms, changing rooms and a stable block to the rear. Despite being used by Canton Cricket Club, Cardiff Bicycle Club and Canton Rugby Football Club throughout the 1880s, the sheer cost of the venture ensured that the consortium went bust in 1883 and the fixtures and fittings were sold off at auction.

Pontypridd Athletic Club, which operated Taff Vale Park after 1901, were rather more successful in their attempts to turn a single recreation ground into a multi-purpose venue. Originally a patch of waste ground situated next to the Forest Iron Works, it was developed in the early 1890s as the home ground of Pontypridd Rugby Football Club (RFC) and was known initially as the Taff Vale grounds. Extensive work on the site before the start of the 1891 season encouraged the use of the more formal and high-quality term 'park'. Writing in the *Glamorgan Free Press* in March 1891, one local correspondent described what could be seen:

> *On arriving at the field an animated sight presented itself. A large assemblage was arranged as to represent the three sides of a rectangle, the space having a goal at each end [...] besides the human fringe, of which I have spoken, a considerable number of sightseers were accommodated with seats and feet protectors in the grandstand. The stand is a decided advantage since it allows ladies to be present and provides an almost certain immunity from bronchic affections to weak and delicate mortals who, rather than sit or stand on damp ground for an hour or so, would be constrained to stay away.*[2]

Pontypridd RFC remained at Taff Vale Park for a decade until the ownership of the ground passed to the athletics syndicate and their efforts to construct a cinder racing track for running and cycling interfered with the size and quality of the rugby pitch. The departure of the club proved to be the catalyst for a remarkable run of athletics, cycling, professional soccer, rugby league and eventually baseball and boxing at the ground. Within a year of taking over, some eleven separate sports were being regularly hosted there.[3] Top runners and cyclists from across Europe and America took part in events at Pontypridd and Taff Vale Park was hailed as the sporting mecca of the Valleys. In an interview with the *Glamorgan Free Press* in October 1903, David Williams, a district councillor and member of the Pontypridd Athletic Club, noted the need to shield the ground from the gaze of those who did not pay their entry fee to ensure its future success. 'We should like to see the ground protected better by larger trees', he explained, 'as we have seen such a very large and appreciative crowd of spectators on the Newport-Caerphilly railway embankment and on the surrounding hills who seem to thoroughly enjoy themselves at

The Valleys' premier sporting venue: Taff Vale Park. Transformed from waste ground left by the local iron works, Taff Vale Park has variously been the home of Pontypridd RFC, Pontypridd AFC, Pontypridd RLFC, greyhound racing, speedway, professional cycling, athletics and pedestrianism, whippet racing, baseball and boxing. Shown above as it was in 1959, the ground had ceased to be a major sporting venue; the photograph to the right, however, gives a sense of the ground in its heyday.

the cost of others'.[4] In some of the more high-profile boxing matches that took place in the 1920s, the owners of Taff Vale Park put up cloth screens to prevent onlookers on the mountains and railway embankments.

Victory in the Powderhall races at Taff Vale Park, August 1911. Professional foot racing began at Taff Vale Park in 1903 and continued until they transferred to Virginia Park, Caerphilly, in 1930. Named after the annual 110m race that took place at the Powderhall Stadium in Edinburgh, the races attracted runners from across Britain, Europe and North America and were a popular highlight of the sporting calendar.

The diversity of sports available at Taff Vale Park provided the basis for its success but, even at its height, the ground never featured more than a single grandstand and as a result was extremely vulnerable to the changing fortunes of its primarily working-class audience. The transfer of Powderhall races to Virginia Park in Caerphilly in 1930 brought about the closure of Taff Vale Park as a commercial venue and it was sold the following year to Pontypridd Education Committee for use as a schools playing field. Although boxing and other sports continued to be held there, it had ceased to be a major venue. With the foundation of Merthyr Town in 1909, Cardiff City in 1910 and Swansea Town, Mid-Rhondda and Newport County in 1912, top-flight soccer (and sport more generally) in south Wales was coming of age and stadiums were quickly replacing recreation grounds.

Stadium Dreams

Sports grounds in the nineteenth century tended to be relatively simple (albeit enclosed) spaces. Typically, cricket clubs constructed a pavilion on their ground but little else in terms of on-site facilities. The sheer popularity of rugby and soccer in the

last quarter of the century and the financial success of clubs such as Cardiff, Newport, Swansea and Wrexham encouraged a different form of arena: the modern stadium. Early grandstand structures were wooden and took their cues from the temporary stands erected at fairs or those present at racecourses. By the Edwardian period, advances in design and demands for permanence had given rise to metal grandstands with the potential for multi-tiered facilities. Typically, stands in the Victorian period were built along one side of the ground only (usually the touchline) with the others landscaped into the famous 'bob banks'. As the club developed, stands were built on the parallel touchline and eventually behind the goals. These transformed grounds from the elliptical shape popular in the Edwardian period to the rectangular design more typical in the second half of the twentieth century.[5]

The permanence of grandstands and terraces was indicative of the rise of sport as a form of popular entertainment after 1870. Many of the stadiums that emerged after that date remain in existence, albeit in modernised form. The Racecourse ground in Wrexham, which has been almost continually the home of

Cricket Pavilion, Pontypridd Park. 95.

Cricket had been played on the Ynysangharad Fields in Pontypridd since the 1870s and in 1926 the ground became Glamorgan's third county ground (Cardiff and Swansea being the two traditional venues). The cricket pavilion provided changing facilities and a small amount of covered viewing space for matches.

Wrexham Football Club since its foundation in 1872, is recognised by the Guinness Book of Records as the oldest in-use international soccer ground in the world. The first international match took place at the ground in 1877 when Wales lost to Scotland 2-0.[6] Originally designed for horse racing, the Racecourse came to be a multi-purpose venue by the mid-nineteenth century with cricket and eventually soccer taking place there along with mass public meetings (especially during coal strikes), local fairs and carnivals. The ground itself took many years to accumulate the traditional paraphernalia of a stadium: during the nineteenth century only the relatively small racing stand next to the Turf Hotel provided sheltered accommodation for spectators. In the absence of a properly enclosed space, the club secured early on the right to eject those who had not paid for their ticket on match days. By the Edwardian period, the club's finances were sufficiently robust to afford to develop the ground properly in the contemporary style. A new stand was built parallel to the Turf Hotel and banking built behind the goal ends giving the ground a quasi-elliptical form.

The design of stadiums in the first decade of the twentieth century was greatly influenced by Archibald Leitch whose early work at Ibrox Park in Glasgow in the 1890s soon brought commissions from across England and Wales including at the Arms Park.[7] Leitch developed two primary forms. The rectangular

The oldest in-use international soccer ground in the world, the Racecourse Ground in Wrexham has been used continuously for the game since the 1870s. This photograph, taken by the RAF in 1948, clearly shows the racecourse which gave the stadium its name, the Turf Hotel which has played a key role in the history of Wrexham Football Club and also the raised bank on which spectators stood to watch their team.

Designed by Archibald Leitch, this was what the Arms Park looked like at the very beginning of the twentieth century. Covered extensions to the grandstand of 1885 give way to uncovered enclosures. Then, as now, the highest quality seats with the best view of the pitch were situated along the half-way line and patrons paid accordingly to sit in them.

ground was used in areas where space was limited and the elliptical ground was constructed at those sites where space was more readily available. The Vetch as with Ninian Park has always been a rectangular stadium because of the cramped conditions into which it was originally squeezed whereas the Racecourse enjoyed a great deal of space and so only became rectangular in form as stands were built on all four sides.

The rectangular stadium would eventually prevail given the undulating landscape of most Welsh communities and the superior sightlines that they provide, although the rugby grounds at Abertillery and Pontypool remain elliptical. Nevertheless, the oval enjoyed a resurgence in the late 1920s as a result of greyhound racing and in a number of stadiums across south Wales, this form was preserved or restored to enable racing to take place. At the Arms Park and at Somerton Park in Newport, the once rectangular stadiums were redesigned to provide for the greyhound track and so gained an elliptical form that would

be retained, despite changing fashion, until the 1990s. Similarly, Penydarren Park in Merthyr Tydfil did not become rectangular in form until the 1970s because of the presence of greyhound racing and (in later years) athletics.

Changes in stadium design were intended to meet the needs of spectators and to encourage wide sections of society to attend matches. The first stand at the Arms Park was constructed in the summer of 1881. A simple, wooden structure, it was demolished a few years later to make way for a grandstand designed to capitalise on the then popularity of Cardiff Rugby Football Club. An additional new stand was built in 1887 to further meet demand. By the end of the decade, the Arms Park had taken on many of the characteristics of a stadium, the enclosed nature of the ground had succeeded in keeping out 'the rabble'.[8] By 1891, physical accommodation for spectators had reached a capacity of 6,000 with standing room on the touchlines for many thousands more.[9] By the early part of the twentieth century, further

The home ground of Pontypool RFC as it was in 1950. Taken by the RAF, this photograph illustrates the tranquillity of Pontypool Park in comparison to the industrialised town spreading into the distance.

The Arms Park grandstand of 1885 packed with spectators before kick-off. Replacing the 1881 stand, this marked the ambitious future of the ground and Welsh rugby itself.

improvements to the stadium saw the number of seats in the grandstand reach 1,800 and twenty-five tier terraces constructed around the sides. These improvements had cost nearly £2,000.

The crowning glory of the Edwardian period was the multi-tiered and multi-purpose pavilion constructed in 1904. Providing dressing rooms and training areas for both the cricket and rugby clubs, it was hailed as a significant step forward particularly for players and officials. Club historian (and secretary) Charles Arthur observed that 'the new pavilion proved of considerable value in the training of players and their comfort generally and the wonder is how the club did without one for so long'. The 1904 pavilion was architecturally impressive: castellated effects including two

turrets added to the majestic façade with its raised balcony and covered seating area underneath. It was also a practical building with an adjoining stable for the use of the groundsman's horse; yet by 1933 it had become surplus to the requirements of the rugby club (and the Welsh Rugby Union) and when the north stand was constructed over in the 1933-34 season, the pavilion was dismantled and moved elsewhere.

Work on the north side of the rugby ground at the Arms Park was made possible by the investment of the Arms Park (Cardiff) Greyhound Racing Company who paid for not only the laying of a track and the modernisation of internal facilities but also expansion of the ground's capacity. When the greyhound track

This impressive pavilion stood at the Arms Park for thirty years and provided on-site changing facilities for the teams and referee, clubrooms (these had previously been in the Westgate Hotel) and a gymnasium, which could also be used for concerts and dining. When it opened in 1904, players and coaches wondered how they had ever managed without it.

opened in May 1928, the *Western Mail* exclaimed: 'the result is that Cardiff Arms Park is already a far different and far more magnificent spot than it was only a few weeks ago'. These changes came at a time when the Welsh Football Union was engaged in a search for a national rugby ground because of the quality of accommodation at St Helen's and at the Arms Park. Their search resulted in the purchase of the Brewery Field in Bridgend and plans were drawn up for a national stadium on the site. One contemporary commentator reflected:

> *Personally I am all for one central commodious ground at Bridgend. For goodness sake do not condemn the idea because the crowd could not be catered for [...] Just use your imagination*

> *in a normal way and the rest is easy. I quite understand vested interests in Cardiff and Swansea using powerful weapons to pour ridicule on the scheme [...] We want a ground comparable with a Wembley or a Murrayfield. Time will bring it — probably at Bridgend.[10]*

The possibility of a national stadium at Bridgend was soon to prove far-fetched given the improvements to the Arms Park and was not pursued.

Across the city, the other footballing code of Cardiff, which increasingly drew fans away from rugby, began to develop a major sporting venue of its own. Ninian Park, built on top of an old rubbish tip leased from Cardiff Corporation for £90 a year,

By the mid-1930s, the Arms Park was a prominent landmark in Cardiff city centre just as the Millennium Stadium is today. This photograph, taken by Aerofilms in 1932, illustrates the clear difference between the imposing international rugby arena and the open cricket ground. Temperance town, at the bottom of the picture, would be demolished just a couple of years later to make way for the central bus station.

opened on 1st September 1910 with a match between Cardiff City and Aston Villa. At the time of opening, the ground was surrounded on three sides by raised banks and on the western side with a small wooden stand. Cheap and popular, the banks were formed from mounds of earth and rubbish covered with a layer of ashes to help with drainage, and during inclement weather the ashes were often washed away leaving spectators standing amidst household refuse: complaints by those on the banks that they were surrounded by 'corned beef cans, buckets and any old thing' were common. Little wonder that in the early years at Ninian Park, conditions on the banks were regularly reported in the newspapers as being indecent.

Over the course of the inter-war years, Ninian Park underwent several changes as Cardiff City became more successful. Elements of this post-Great War development were strikingly novel: the Canton Stand, which was unveiled in 1920, had benched seating rather than being standing room only, as was common then and for several decades afterwards. The destruction of the original wooden grandstand in January 1937, by a fire apparently started by thieves attempting to steal gate money from the safe, enabled the construction of a permanent brick stand as a replacement. Improvements to the bob bank and other open areas, such as wooden decking and terracing were also forthcoming.

The Vetch, by contrast, suffered not from poor conditions on the terraces but instead from the constrained nature of the site. The field, rented from Swansea Gas Company, had once been used by the local athletic and cycling club who also found the site to be a difficult one to use with the cycling track laid down on the site featuring tighter corners that were far from ideal: as a result, the first season that Swansea Town played at the Vetch the pitch was comprised of cinders. The demolition of the Salvation Army Hall enabled the laying out of a true pitch but still did not leave a great deal of room of further development. The grandstand, with its famous clock, was opened in 1913 and the

double-decker west stand in 1927 but otherwise the ground was enclosed only by fencing. In later years, these would be terraced and eventually covered. Just as at Ninian Park, the open nature of the banks left many fans drenched during bad weather and also in danger of being crushed during well attended matches.

The situation was little better in Aberystwyth. Park Avenue, Aberystwyth Town's home ground, has never been entirely enclosed by a permanent grandstand. Instead, much of the ground has stood open to the elements with only the south stand, which backs onto the river Rheidol, providing shelter for spectators. Prior to being made available to the soccer club, Park Avenue (or the Smithfield as it was previously known) was used by university students for their team sports and had been a commercial tennis ground before that. The university sides had constructed a pavilion on the north side although this was soon demolished by the soccer club since it was better suited to tennis than to soccer fans.

Given the location (not to mention the temperamental weather in west Wales), the Smithfield was prone to often disastrous flooding and one of the club's first actions upon taking hold of the lease was to put in adequate drainage and to lay down a cinder track for spectators to stand on, rather than have paying customers squelching about in the mud. Following the Great War and the return to normal civilian life, the question of solving the issues of flooding at the Smithfield was tackled once again; this time by raising the level of the ground by around four feet using refuse from the infirmary and local sewerage works. As elsewhere, the construction of a grandstand that obscured the previously free view from higher ground (in this case Penparcau Hill) was also high on the agenda along with ticket booths and turnstiles and the proper enclosure of the field. The stand was eventually constructed in 1926 much to the relief of spectators.

In the south Wales valleys, stadiums were constructed in those places where flat land could be acquired relatively easily. Many developed as multi-purpose athletics facilities catering for professional sports such as cycling, soccer and rugby league. Aberdare's Ynys Stadium and Mid-Rhondda Athletic Ground in Tonypandy emerged in the first decade of the twentieth century. Featuring a race track for cycling and running as well as a sports pitch, these grounds fitted the entrepreneurial pattern established by the consortia running Taff Vale Park and Alexandra Park. Yet, amidst the rebellion in Welsh rugby that began in 1907 over the

Cardiff is a city of both footballing codes, of course. Ninian Park, the home of Cardiff City Football Club, developed steadily after 1910 into this impressive stadium photographed by Aerofilms in 1959. Enclosed on all sides with covered grandstands, this was the pinnacle of soccer stadiums in Wales. In the background is the Arms Park with its double-decker north stand.

The Vetch as it was in 1959. Hampered by the cramped location, the Vetch developed slowly after 1912 with just three sides being covered with grandstands. The oldest of these, on the left of the ground in this photograph, opened in 1913 and remained part of the stadium until its recent demolition.

In 1921, by contrast, the Vetch was a ground open to the elements. With a match in progress, this early Aerofilms photograph shows not only the popularity of Swansea Town in its first decade but also the amount of groundwork that had been necessary to raise the ground up out of the view of local houses.

remuneration of players, both the Ynys Stadium and Mid-Rhondda Athletic Ground came to be even more historic. It was in Aberdare that, in front of thousands on New Year's Day 1908, the first ever rugby league international between Wales and New Zealand took place. The home side won by nine points to eight. A few months later, in April 1908, Wales met England for the first

time at the Mid-Rhondda ground and won 35-18. Built by the Mid-Rhondda Athletic Company and opened on Easter Monday 1903, the ground had cost £3,000 and eventually established itself as one of the leading athletics venues in the coalfield. As with Taff Vale Park, both the Ynys and Mid-Rhondda were municipalised in the 1930s and given over to local schools for use as playing fields.

Kick off by local celebrities was a common way of drawing large crowds and marking significant matches. This photograph shows Ted Lewis, boxing promoter and all-round Mr Sportsman of Pontypridd, kicking off at Taff Vale Park in about 1920.

A New Hope

In the late 1920s, with Britain in the grip of severe economic downturn, few industries appeared robust enough to provide an alternative means of employment for those who had lost their jobs in manufacturing and heavy industry. Across Britain, the leisure industry during the Depression rose substantially and the number of people employed in cinemas, theatres and in sports stadiums and arenas went up accordingly. The effects were no less apparent in Wales, albeit on a smaller scale than was true of England and Scotland. This was in large part due to the rising number of recreational amenities, stadiums and sports arenas that were built in the 1920s and 1930s. From the groundsman at

a welfare ground in the valleys being paid a gratuity of a few shillings a week to the scores of people employed at the Welsh White City stadium in Cardiff, sport provided not just entertainment but vital economic lifelines as well. In Cardiff, for example, when the arrival of greyhound racing was announced in September 1927, queues of men began appearing along Sloper Road in the hope of gaining a day's work on the construction site. This desperate need for work in the main city of Wales caught the attention of national journalists and in the pages of the *Manchester Guardian*, readers were told that 'for several days hundreds of men have congregated in Sloper Road in the hopes of being employed, several of them presenting themselves even

Advertising events at racetracks was not limited to handbills passed to customers, billboards on junctions or in the columns of the local newspaper. At Hawthorn Racecourse in Pontypridd, promoters hired vans to carry champion greyhounds into the town to show off their prized racers to would-be spectators.

before daybreak'.[11] Both tracks in the city — the other opened in the Arms Park — employed local firms to undertake the laying out of the tracks and materials were bought from companies such as the Aberthaw Cement Factory.[12]

Greyhound racing and speedway began to have a presence in Wales in the late 1920s, their arrival came at a time when economic confidence was low and many communities were in desperate need of inward investment. Though few tracks were built from scratch — the Welsh White City is an exception — the laying out of a dog track meant thousands of pounds was spent in the local area or in the stadium itself. The Arms Park Greyhound Racing Company were paying £1,000 a year in rent

to Cardiff Athletic Club to sub-let the Arms Park in the early 1930s whilst the conversion of Taff Vale Park had cost around £25,000.[13] Within ten years of the Welsh White City opening in 1928, at least ten new race tracks had opened across south Wales. Aside from the Cardiff tracks, there was a racing circuit in Aberdare, Barry, Caerphilly, Merthyr Tydfil, Newport, Pontypridd, Swansea and Tredegar and the prospect of several others. The new circuits enjoyed varying success in the years before the Second World War and at times, particularly in the 1950s, after the war had ended. The concentration of tracks throughout the coalfield in the 1920s and early 1930s, however, was never regained despite the construction of new ones such

The only major sporting venue built in Cardiff in the inter-war years, the Welsh White City greyhound stadium was situated along Sloper Road and opened in 1928. This photograph, taken by Aerofilms in 1933, captures the stadium near the height of its popularity. The board to the left of the track was the totalisator (or tote) machine which was central to betting on the dogs.

as that in Cymmer in the Rhondda. The last dog races in Cardiff took place in 1977 prior to the redevelopment of the Arms Park into the Wales National Stadium. After a few more years of dog racing at Somerton Park, the sport declined surviving only at Bedwellty Greyhound Stadium near Ystrad Mynach and at Fforestfach in Swansea. Both have now closed.

The post-war revival of speedway was more dramatic. The short-lived Cardiff Dragons thrilled audiences in the early 1950s

but the failure to convince Cardiff Council to allow races to take place at Maindy Stadium meant the financial burden of constructing a new stadium on Penarth Road on the outskirts of the city. Although audiences did travel to watch, the lack of a city centre venue took its toll and by 1953 the team had disbanded. A brief attempt to reform at a track built in the shadow of Neath Abbey was also unsuccessful and it was not until the formation of the Newport Wasps in 1964 that speedway gained a firm

The home ground of Newport County from 1912 until it finally closed during the 1992–93 season, Somerton Park is now a housing estate. Shown here in a photograph taken by Aerofilms in 1966, the ground features its greyhound track (racing began here in 1932). Notice that the grandstands obscure the view from the local houses.

Taken in 1959, this Aerofilms photograph shows the greyhound racing track at **Cymmer** in the Rhondda, which was part of a new wave of dog tracks that opened in post-war Wales. The track, shown on the left, did not survive very long and the site was turned into housing by the end of the 1960s.

footing. With a base at Somerton Park, the team survived until 1977 when the fortunes of speedway on a national level were waning. In more recent years, the sport has experienced a resurgence in popularity. The Newport Wasps were revived in 1997 and continue to race in the British leagues at their home track at Queensway Meadows. High-profile races also take place annually at the Millennium stadium.

Speedway and greyhound racing were two of the three major commercial sports to arrive in Britain in the 1920s and 1930s. The third, ice hockey, never made it to Wales despite plans by the British Ice Hockey Association to extend a franchise to Cardiff in the early 1940s and simultaneous plans by Cardiff Council to construct an ice rink as part of its intended sports complex on Wood Street. These were inevitably scuppered by the outbreak

Situated on the outskirts of Cardiff, Penarth Road Speedway Stadium existed for a short time in the 1950s and provided, for the very first time, a dedicated venue for dirt-track races and the home ground of the Cardiff Dragons team. This photograph, taken by the RAF in July 1950, shows the stadium shortly after it opened.

of war in 1939 and though there were renewed calls for an ice rink in the 1950s, ice hockey did not gain a foothold until 1986 with the construction of the Wales National Ice Rink in central Cardiff.[14] Costing £2.5 million, the rink became home to the phenomenally successful Cardiff Devils who played their first

match, in front of 2,500 people, against the Ashfield Islanders in November of that year. The Wales National Ice Rink remained open until 2006 when it was demolished along with surrounding buildings as part of the St David's 2 shopping centre development on the Hayes.

Long before the establishment of the Cardiff Devils, pushing the puck on the ice was a popular winter activity and a reasonably large, if marginalised, sport in Britain. This photograph, taken in Cwmbach in 1969, shows the rudimentary way in which ice hockey was played. No padding or expensive sticks or even ice skates for this group of children!

The New Religion

Since the Second World War, the sports stadium has become the iconic building of the modern age. Able to encapsulate the collective identities of entire nations, these structures have few parallels in contemporary society. Consider the Wales National Stadium. Begun in 1967 and built from materials made in Wales, it exemplified the strong relationship between industrial life and cultural life and encapsulated post-war economic optimism in a manner akin to the *Cool Cymru* phenomenon that accompanied the opening of the Millennium Stadium and the Rugby World Cup in 1999. The latter stadium, with its pioneering technology and contemporary design, represents a different Wales from that of its predecessor. No longer rooted in its industrial past, this is a nation confident for entirely different reasons: young, vigorous and energetic. A metaphor for what might be achieved rather than what had, for better or worse, been done in generations past.

Few of the historic stadiums have survived long into the twenty-first century. By 2011, Stradey Park, the Vetch and Ninian Park had all been demolished and the flight from the restrictions of historic venues was in full swing right across the sporting landscape. Since the professionalisation of rugby in the mid-1990s, the only regional side to still play at their historic ground is the Newport-Gwent Dragons. The others have all moved on. The Liberty Stadium, Parc-y-Scarlets and the City of Cardiff Stadium all symbolise the modern professional nature of sport in twenty-first century Wales. Indeed, viewed from the end of the first decade of the twenty-first century, the loss of sporting facilities in a wave of modernisation in the 1980s and 1990s was very much part of this trend albeit on a more parochial scale. Closure of open-air swimming baths across Wales and the conversion of a

The old and the new side-by-side: Ninian Park and the City of Cardiff Stadium. By the early twenty-first century, older stadiums could no longer meet the demands placed on them by top-flight professional sport. With little space to expand and develop, clubs began to move away from their traditional home grounds to purpose-built and wholly modern stadiums. This photograph, taken by the Royal Commission's aerial reconnaissance unit in 2008, captured these changes beautifully.

Rodney Parade in Newport as it appeared in the 1950s. Shown here at its height, the grounds hosted cricket, soccer, rugby, tennis, bowls and athletics. The cricket ground was later sold off and Maindy Primary School was built on the site whilst, for the most part, the rest of the facilities remain intact. By the time this photograph was taken, as many as 28,000 people could watch matches at the rugby ground!

The **SWALEC** Stadium has transformed top-flight cricket in Wales and it is now possible to hold international test matches in Cardiff. With its open stands, the **SWALEC** Stadium is unique amongst the current trend of sporting venues that have tended towards fully-covered grandstands.

small fraction of what once existed is strong evidence of a lack of care taken with Wales's twentieth-century built heritage. This has, of course, been a traditional part of the developing sporting landscape and the period since 1980 is therefore not entirely unusual, rather it is the level of loss and destruction that marks it out as separate from trends established in the previous century.

Major changes to Wales' network of stadiums began to take place in the late 1960s, beginning with the complete transformation of the Arms Park. This resulted in the construction of a separate ground for Cardiff RFC on the site of the century-old cricket ground. The cricketers themselves moved to Sophia Gardens, thereby satisfying a long-standing desire of their own to

move to a dedicated site. The catalyst to these changes was the suggestion by the Welsh Rugby Union that it might move international rugby out of Cardiff to a dedicated site in Bridgend (a replay of its abortive efforts in the 1930s). Faced with the financially disastrous loss of international match days and a severe loss of prestige, the city council engaged with the WRU and Cardiff Athletic Club and drew up the plans to develop the rugby stadium at the Arms Park into an independent international venue. The building work took almost fifteen years to complete and the Wales National Stadium was finally opened in 1984 costing the WRU over £9 million. The modernised stadium quickly became one of the most iconic stadiums in the world. With a brutalist design rendered in concrete, it was both striking but remarkably simple. Only three sides were ever covered leaving the terraces of the east stand open to the elements. This was an old-fashioned aspect to the ground which connected with the amateur ethos of the game during the stadium's heyday.

The new cricket stadium at Sophia Gardens opened in 1967 with a match against the touring Indians. The ground itself was little improved on the old Arms Park wicket and the stands and enclosures were merely transplanted from one site to the other. Through the 1970s and 1980s, these decades-old stands remained little altered and the home of Welsh cricket appeared relatively shabby in comparison with the major cricket grounds of the English counties. Given their age these facilities were 'notorious for splinters'.[15] Modernisation of the ground began in 2005 with the installation of permanent floodlighting and between 2006 and 2008 the entire stadium was reconstructed providing new stands, a state-of-the-art media centre and modern facilities for staff and players. Now known as the SWALEC Stadium, the twenty-first century cricket ground at Sophia Gardens has reached the test standard of the major English stadiums and hosted the first test match of the 2009 Ashes.

Since the early 1990s, the reconstruction of major stadiums across Britain has taken place. Following the recommendations of the Taylor Report into the Hillsborough Disaster of 1989, they have been converted into all-seater venues. Accordingly, modern grounds such as Parc-y-Scarlets, the Liberty Stadium, City of Cardiff Stadium, SWALEC Stadium and the Millennium Stadium have no standing places whatsoever. Entirely enclosed with seated stands, these stadiums represent the pinnacle of development over the previous century and signify the commercial importance of professional rugby, professional soccer and professional cricket. The most significant of these stadiums is the Millennium Stadium. Built in the late 1990s as the showpiece ground of the 1999 Rugby World Cup, today it encapsulates the confidence of Wales in the era of devolution.

The most recognisable arena in Wales: the Millennium Stadium. Opened for the 1999 Rugby World Cup, it has served as a high-profile and extremely successful replacement for the Wales National Stadium. Visible behind are the terraces of the Arms Park, the dedicated home of Cardiff RFC since the removal of Glamorgan to Sophia Gardens in the 1960s, and the hardy bowling green which is now the last piece of the athletics grounds of the Victorian town.

CHAPTER VI:

The Nation as Playground

I have a South Wales view of mountains. I want them of a size I can live on and walk on. We have them in Glamorgan. One after another, small, rough ranges of classic line, shortish and utterly accessible, like the dark, exuberant Celts who fiddle about at their feet.

Gwyn Thomas, *A Welsh Eye* (1964)

The drama of the natural landscape of Wales – particularly its mountains – has drawn tourists for centuries and the creation of a version of the 'Highland Romance' in the late eighteenth century has served to frame its appreciation by visitors. It had not always been this way. 'The starkness of Welsh scenery', writes the historian Simon Schama, 'had long been imagined in London as the epitome of barbaric rudeness, and the language spoken by the natives the phonetic equivalent'.[1] As attitudes softened and a new appreciation of the landscape emerged in the course of the eighteenth century, the 'Wild Wales' that still exercises a profound influence on popular imagery was born, accompanied by a Romantic mythology that could match that created by Sir Walter Scott for Scotland. The Welsh countryside has come to be seen since the late eighteenth century as a playground of great importance to local people and tourists alike. Whilst the people of the industrialised south, in Lloyd George's view, had been given over to a morbid footballism, the rural character of central and northern counties was such that 'the inhabitants take practically no interest in horse-races nor in the achievements of football teams'.[2]

Exploiting these divisions for tourism has transformed the countryside into a natural playground designed to meet the needs and expectations of those living in urban Britain. Quaint houses, little tea shops and 'unspoiled' villages fuel a vision of the countryside which relies much more on myth than on the often difficult realities of life in more isolated communities. Yet, with its proximity to major cities in western England such as Liverpool, Birmingham and Bristol as well as Welsh urban areas, the three National Parks have gained an importance in the development of outdoor activities to parallel the Lake District or to the Highlands. Steady streams of tourists seeking respite from the urban sprawl have found it in the rugged, wild landscapes of Snowdonia or the Brecon Beacons. It was in north Wales that pioneering hostellers founded Britain's first youth hostel in the 1930s; it was on the wide estuary at Aberdyfi that Britain's first outward bound school was opened in the 1940s; and it was to protect the beauty and majesty of Gower that in the 1960s it was designated Britain's first Area of Outstanding Natural Beauty (AONB).[3]

The changing relationship between residents and tourists and the natural landscape can be explored through many different aspects of leisure activity from walking and cycling to fell-running and driving. Each sheds light on the history of the countryside as a playground for largely urban tourists and reveals much about the imposition of urban ideas of a rural idyll over the realities of living in often deprived communities. The freedom and calm expected of the countryside was (and is) contrasted with the hustle and bustle of the city and ensured the development of the idea of rural life being 'simpler' than that lived in the towns and cities of urban Britain. The desire for greater freedom sent many into the countryside where there seemed to be fewer rules and regulations and certainly fewer of the entrapments of modern society.

In post-war Wales, public parks were reconciled to all manner of sporting activity. This photograph, taken in 1957, shows a group of cyclists during the annual bicycle races that took place in Aberdare Park in the 1950s, 1960s and 1970s.

Rambling Hills

Romantic tourism emerged in the late eighteenth and early nineteenth centuries and took its inspiration from the engagement with the landscape by artists, writers, poets and

Although formal playing fields were laid out in communities in the south Wales valleys, as this photograph of Penrhiwceiber taken by Aerofilms in 1964 illustrates, the forests and abundant open space on the hillsides continued to attract locals and visitors alike.

musicians. Hill walking, which later developed into more organised leisure activities such as rambling and mountaineering, was the first means by which Romantic tourists including the artist J.M.W. Turner and the writer Benjamin Heath Malkin enjoyed the wilder landscapes of Gwynedd, Brecon and the then largely rural Glamorgan valleys. Tourists were often drawn from wealthier backgrounds (since they had the greatest amount of leisure time) but not exclusively. One of the most famous descriptions, which aimed at encapsulating the lost world of the Glamorgan valleys in the midst of rapid industrialisation, is that written by William Thomas, a Nonconformist minister traditionally known by his bardic name Glanffrwd. Born in Ynysybwl in March 1843,

Glanffrwd lived much of his life away from Llanwonno but was nevertheless extremely sensitive to the remarkable changes effected in the parish by the coal rush. In a series of articles published in the Aberdare newspaper *Tarian y Gweithiwr* (The Workman's Shield) in the 1880s, Glanffrwd described activities such as Ynysybwl Fair and many of the lively characters who lived in the area in the first half of the nineteenth century.[4]

The hamlet into which William Thomas was born contained a small number of cottages, outlying farms, a mill, a school and a pub. The social lives of its residents were dominated by the patterns of agricultural production with annual fairs in March which brought the entire community together. Sporting activity including handball took place in the vicinity of the local pub with team games having their own dedicated pitch. Similar traditions thrived in the rural hamlets throughout Wales. By the end of the century, Ynysybwl had been transformed into a 'compact village with a population of almost five thousand'.[5] Yet despite this, for at least a generation, the community maintained earlier patterns of recreation and continued to celebrate key events in the rural calendar including the annual fair. Teachers complained of low attendance when children were sent to pick blackberries or were taken to local horse-racing events by their parents. The schools were simply closed for the March fair because attendance would have been so slight.[6]

On the other side of the mountain, in Penrhiwceiber and Mountain Ash, the Irish-Welsh novelist Joseph Keating was born in April 1871. In his autobiography he remembers the community being 'a charming, pastoral village [...] set in a wooded valley and sheltered by wonderful mountains'.[7] Just as Glanffrwd found solace and comfort wandering the hills near Ynysybwl so too did Keating find in the hills of the lower Cynon Valley the freedom that he craved. 'During school-time', he writes, 'I was up in the mountains. I had often sat on our doorstep looking up at the hills [...] Up there I was out of reach of punishment or restraint'.[8] The freedom of the countryside on the fringes of industrialisation remained a powerful attraction right through the nineteenth and

The upland ranges of Gwynedd have long drawn walkers and mountaineers. This photograph, taken at Tryfan in Snowdonia, gives a sense of the appeal of the challenging climb and the majesty of the surroundings.

twentieth centuries. For young adults, walks along quiet country roads in the early evening formed an essential part of courting. Edith Davies from Ynysybwl recalls:

The young girls in flowered hats, sprig muslin dresses and white shoes and stockings. They strolled in groups, chattering and laughing together, lovely as nymphs. They were apparently oblivious of the straw-boatered, dapper young men who strolled amongst them with a feigned nonchalance, but at the same time keeping a sharp look-out for the girl of their fancy [...] many a happy marriage resulted from a summer evening romance begun on a twilit Grovers Road.[9]

If the mountains and hills provided freedom for children and a scenic backdrop to romance for some adults, for others the mountains presented different challenges. For them, walking to the summit on long-established paths was no longer thrilling enough and with mountaineering in the Alps emerging as a popular pastime in the middle part of the nineteenth century, English climbers sought ranges in Britain to practice their skills.[10] As a result the higher peaks of Wales, and Snowdonia in particular, came to be a popular destination. The lower height of the mountains in south Wales meant that they were largely ignored by serious mountaineers.[11] Charles Evans, a leading Himalayan mountaineer, explained the appeal of Snowdonia in these terms:

Eryri has a character which the mountaineer recognizes at once as akin to that of higher ranges, and so climbers often describe its mountains as 'real mountains': the landscape is bare and rugged; the traces of the work of ice are everywhere to be seen; some of the tops, which are often sharp, can only be reached and traversed by ways that are steep and rough; many of the ridges are rocky and broken, and give a sense of height because the slopes fall steeply from them on either side, and some of the high ground, when transformed in winter by snow, may be safely accessible only to experienced and properly equipped mountaineers.[12]

Though Welsh mountains formed an essential part of the development of mountaineering in Britain, it was not a sport that garnered a great deal of attention from the Welsh who viewed their mountains not as a challenge of physical endurance or leisure but as a place of work. 'We Welsh', complained the historian of the *Urdd Gobaith Cymru* in the 1970s, 'wasted our time selling bottles of pop to them [the English climbers] at the bottom'.[13] By contrast, 'It was the English [climbers] who appeared to use the Welsh mountains to develop and invent the sport of mountaineering and its progeny, rock climbing'.[14] But watching intrepid adventurers scramble to the summit of Snowdon from the perspective of the refreshment stand at the bottom was not going to hold the interest of the Welsh for long and by the end of the nineteenth century Welsh mountaineering clubs had been set up as well.

Typically, tourists to the peaks of Snowdonia settled in Llandudno before making their way inland on the train towards mountain villages such as Capel Curig, Betws-y-Coed and Blaenau Ffestiniog. This was to be a well-organised leisure activity with institutions such as the Llandudno Snowdonian Club (later Llandudno Mountaineering Club) and, in 1898, the Climbers' Club which exercised considerable influence on the future direction of the sport in Wales and on Welsh mountains. Members of these clubs regularly wrote of their excursions and routes in the local, national and specialist press. On Boxing Day, 1892, one group of members from the Llandudno Club set off to reach the summit of Foel-Fras where they 'sat down on the ice in the shade of Talyfan' and ate the remainders of Christmas dinner, which they had dragged along with them in a picnic basket.[15]

The popularity of mountaineering in Snowdonia by the 1890s resulted in the construction of the Snowdon Mountain Railway, which took its inspiration from similar facilities in Switzerland.[16] Work began in 1894 and was completed by 1896 having cost over £60,000. The official opening of the railway took place on Monday 6 April 1896 but was marred by an accident, which saw the engine leave the tracks and topple over the precipice. Panic set in amongst some passengers and one man — Ellis Roberts, an hotelier from Llanberis — sustained such injuries in leaping from the train that he died the following day.[17] With passengers having reached a degree of safety, a second train, which had been mistakenly sent down the mountain in the fog, crashed into the first. Newspapers across Britain reported the shocking events and the railway closed for twelve months whilst upgrades and safety improvements, including the gripper rail, were made. It reopened on 19 April 1897.[18]

Many early youth hostels were laid out in converted buildings such as this former Victorian school house in Corris. Opened as a youth hostel in the mid-1960s, it was closed by the YHA in 1991 but reopened the following year as an independent hostel and bunkhouse.

Then, as now, many of the villages that provided ready access to the mountain paths such as Llanberis and Betws-y-Coed thrived on tourism and numerous hotels, lodges, and other alpine facilities were established by enterprising individuals or by the clubs themselves. The first 'climbers' hut' in Britain was established at an old cottage called Helyg in the Ogwen Valley and opened to members of the Climbers' Club on 31 October 1925. Further huts have opened throughout Snowdonia and other popular destinations for mountaineers and hill walkers in subsequent years. The Climbers' Club itself operates two others, both of which are in the Llanberis Pass: Cwm Glas, which opened in 1948 and Ynys Ettws, which opened in 1950. These bases enabled climbers to spend longer periods of time in the mountains at much cheaper rates than in hotels: a stay in Helyg in the early 1930s cost between 1s and 1s 6d for members and 2s for non-members per night.[19]

The provision of club accommodation in the countryside mirrored developments in Germany with the emergence of the youth hostel movement providing cheap and simple facilities to encourage travel into more isolated parts. Spreading to the UK in the 1930s, youth hostels transformed the potential for young people to travel into the countryside on holiday. The first youth hostel in the United Kingdom opened at Pennant Hall, near Llanrwst in the Conwy Valley, on Christmas Eve 1930.[20] Although short-lived — Llanrwst closed in 1931 as a result of difficulties with its water supply — the youth hostel movement thrived, and by the end of the year over seventy hostels had opened across England and Wales.

A few of the earliest hostels remain in use. Idwal Cottage, near Bethesda in Gwynedd, was one of those that opened in 1931 and is amongst the oldest youth hostels in Britain today. Laid out in a former quarry manager's house, the hostel served as a base from which to explore the rugged and wild landscape of Snowdonia. On the other side of the national park, in Dolgellau, the YHA discovered a dilapidated house that had formerly been the King's Mill and set about converting it for use as a hostel. Opened in 1937 and extended in 1938-39, the King's Mill was requisitioned during the Second World War for use by an evacuated nursery from Birmingham. It eventually reopened as a hostel in March 1945 and has remained in use ever since.[21]

The rapid expansion of the YHA demonstrated its importance to certain young people and its ability to satisfy their desire to go on cheap holidays. By 1937, the YHA had over 70,000 members and some 275 hostels. Today, by contrast, it has over 200,000 members but only 200 hostels and bunkhouses (around thirty of these in Wales).[22] But it was not a universal attraction and could not compete with spectator sports and drinking. With members encouraged to arrive on foot, via public transport or on a bicycle, going to youth hostels required planning and more spare time than simply going to the match on a Saturday or Wednesday afternoon. In the view of historian Richard Holt, 'most workers preferred the security and familiarity of "the match" on a Saturday afternoon. Sunday morning was spent sleeping off the excesses of Saturday night'.[23] This point is echoed by Richard Hoggart who suggests that one of the flaws of the Cyclists' Touring Club was that rather than cycling 30 miles or more, 'many young people insist that they "like their bed" on a Sunday morning'.[24]

Where supply met demand. Bicycle shops such as this one in Carmarthen could be found across Wales by the early twentieth century. Providing the latest models, club uniforms, maps and guidebooks, tools and repairs these shops were a vital part of cycling's growing appeal.

The Freedom of Wheels

The advent of mass cycling in Britain in the 1880s and 1890s prompted a boom in cycling clubs, cycle racing and cycle tourism.[25] Maps and handbooks were produced detailing the best routes through countryside, hotels promoted themselves as cyclist-friendly by offering special rates for club members, and shops providing equipment and repair facilities could be found in towns, cities, and even in more out-of-the-way villages in order to meet growing demand from almost all parts of society. Enthusiasm was particularly notable along the north Wales coast where a combination of relatively flat routes (albeit with magnificent views of Snowdonia) and proximity to large urban centres such as Liverpool and Manchester created Wales' first cycling hotspot. Organised club activity in the region was led by Rhyl Cycling Club, which formed in 1878, and tourists from across Britain were encouraged to sample the delights of north Wales instead of flocking to the continent. 'Wales is absolutely unsurpassed as a touring ground for cyclists', enthused the journal *Cycling*, 'and he who goes there once goes many times'.[26]

In south Wales, several centres of cycling emerged. Swansea experienced a boom in cycling activity in the 1880s with Oystermouth Road a particular favourite amongst enthusiasts there with clubs such as the Swansea Harriers and the Argyle Cycling Club providing organised runs. By 1891, Cardiff had three

The popularity of cycling in the late-1880s and 1890s led to a boom in the number of clubs across Wales. This picture shows Bridgend Cycling Club in 1889. The stylised uniforms with caps and badges are illustrative of the formal approach taken by clubs at that time.

The Cynon valley has produced several of Wales' leading cyclists. This photograph shows Arthur Linton whose achievements on the track, particularly in France, earned him significant fame before his death from typhoid in 1896. He was 24 years old.

clubs — Cardiff, Cardiff United and Roath — with a combined total of 400 members.[27] Within just a few years, there were seven clubs including the Cardiff 100 Miles and Cardiff Jockey clubs.[28] The latter club, which formed in April 1891, had a membership of 180 by the end of the 1894.[29] When the south Wales district of the National Cyclists' Union was formed in 1892, the founding members came from across the region with clubs such as the Swansea Harriers, Aberdare, Aberaman Stars, Neath United, Mountain Ash, and Aberystwyth joining with the Cardiff and

Cardiff Jockeys.[30] It was from the coalfield, and particularly the Cynon Valley, that several world-class cyclists emerged in the 1890s including Jimmy Michael and the Linton Brothers Arthur and Tom.[31] So generally popular was the sport that at the National Eisteddfod held in Pontypridd in 1893 there was a five guinea prize for the best model bicycle.[32]

The overall popularity of cycling in this period was aided by technical improvements at the end of the 1880s. John Dunlop's invention of the pneumatic tyre in 1888 and the manufacture of the safety bicycle with its equal wheel sizes from the middle of the decade meant that cycling ceased to be an athletic pursuit only for young men. Lighter machines made longer journeys possible and mass manufacture enabled a wider range of people to afford bicycles than had been the case in earlier decades.[33] As a consequence, the bicycle became a means of transport, a symbol of freedom, and a machine for sport in various forms from circuit racing to the cross-country, hundred mile runs from Cardiff to Builth Wells and back organised by the Cardiff 100 Miles Cycling Club took place each year.

Although many cycling clubs were local affairs, the Welsh countryside was an important part of the network of touring facilities that were established following the creation of the Bicycle Touring Club in 1878. Renamed the Cyclists' Touring Club (CTC) in 1883, the organisation, which boasted a membership of over 10,000, moved headquarters from Harrogate to London and promoted cycling on a national scale.[34] By the start of the twentieth century, the CTC had a membership of around 60,000, although this had fallen back to around 15,000 by the outbreak of the Great War in 1914. Experiencing a continued decline in members through the war, the CTC were able to reverse slowly the situation through the 1920s and 1930s, reaching nearly 37,000 members by 1939. Similar trends were apparent at the local level, particularly in north Wales, which had been a stronghold of cycling in the nineteenth century. Whereas a district association of the CTC had been formed in Glamorgan in 1900 and then expanded to cover Cardiff and south Wales in 1920, a north Wales equivalent was formed only in 1929. The latter collapsed in 1938 leaving no regional representation for members of the CTC in the north of the country.[35]

Individual membership of the CTC entitled a cyclist to discounted meals, refreshments, accommodation, and bicycle repair at designated headquarters across Britain (although the rates varied between Scotland and England and Wales). Headquarters were often hotels, public houses or inns and were situated in major stopping points along the most popular tourist routes. Designated headquarters were not without controversy. Many were relatively expensive and beyond the means of lower middle-class and working-class cyclists escaping towns at the weekend. The negotiated rate of 7s 6d for a set of three meals and a single bed at CTC headquarters in England and Wales in the 1890s, for example, was relatively high and prompted complaints

The Cyclists' Touring Club.

3, CRAVEN HILL,
LONDON, W.2.

DEAR SIR (OR MADAM),

I am now preparing for publication the 1932 edition of this Club's Handbook, and am desirous of knowing whether you wish to make any changes in your tariff, which at present is as follows:—

	£	s	d.
1.—SINGLE-BEDDED ROOM		3	-
2.—BED AND BREAKFAST		5	-
3.—PLAIN TEA (tea, bread and butter, greenstuff in season, preserve and cake)		1	-
4.—LUNCH		1	6
5.—DINNER		2	-
6.—BATH. Hot........s.........d. Cold........s........d.			
7.—TERMS PER DAY (inclusive)			
8.—TERMS PER WEEK (inclusive)	1	15	-

Please return the attached post card, which will ensure your establishment remaining in our Handbook.

Note. No further communication will be sent, and failure to return the card will mean deletion from our list.

Yours faithfully,
G. HERBERT STANCER, *Secretary*.

In common with the AA and the RAC in later years, membership of the Cyclists' Touring Club provided discounts at hotels and guestrooms. This circulation, dating from 1932, shows the rates for one hotel in Presteigne.

from poorer members of the club that it was unaffordable for all.[36] Cost and the choice of particular hotels reflected the wealthy origins of cycle tourism in the nineteenth century and it took many years to shake off Victorian middle-class etiquette even as that section of society began to drift away from the cycling clubs. By the 1920s and 1930s this system of headquarters had been abandoned in favour of a much wider network offering a greater variety of prices to meet the needs of all members.

Hotels, guesthouses and pubs, which provided discounts to members of the Cyclists' Touring Club were emblazoned with the Winged Wheel, the club's logo as the photograph of Llandovery in 1912 (above left) shows. The King's Head Inn, in the centre of the image, has one on the right-hand side of the building. Few of these have survived intact, sadly that at Llandovery has not. The wheel on the Black Lion Hotel in Pontrhydfendigaid is a fine example of one that has.

Headquarters and other sanctioned facilities were typically marked with the distinctive winged wheel emblem of the CTC. Although few of these now survive, former CTC locations in Bala, Cowbridge, Llandysul, Llandeilo, Pontrhydfendigaid and Rhuddlan are still emblazoned with their winged wheel whilst historic photographs of public houses and hotels provide visual evidence of this once extensive network of facilities for cyclists.

Cycle tourism brought increasing numbers of people from across Britain into the countryside. As a result, published material relating to roads, mountains, towns, and the history of the nation began to increase. They reveal not only the wealth of interest in the rural landscape of central and northern counties but also a striking disdain for the industrial communities of the southern coalfield. Whilst acknowledging the importance of its castle, the CTC guide to the roads of the West Midlands and Wales (published in 1931) considers Caerphilly to have been a 'small,

Cycling into the countryside remains a popular form of leisure and the landscape of Wales offers a diverse range of challenges. This photograph shows a group of cyclists from Maesteg Cycling Club on tour in 1938.

drab, industrial town'. Crumlin, a few miles to the east, was a 'good example of natural scenery marred by industrialism', the 'old market town' of Neath was said to have been 'spoiled by industrialism', and Morriston was dismissed as an 'ugly industrial suburb of Swansea'.[37] By contrast, more rural towns and villages were praised for their pleasant appearance and picturesque nature. Conwy is described as 'the most striking and romantic of the ancient towns' and Gower as considerably attractive.[38]

This tendency to reduce Wales to questions of aesthetics rather than of people was decried by H.V. Morton in his popular and much-reprinted *In Search of Wales* originally published in 1932.[39] 'Too many people come to Wales', he lamented, 'to look

at it and go home without the slightest idea that they have encountered an alien culture'.[40] For Morton (and for contemporary travel writers), Wales was as complex as it was beautiful. Travelling through the countryside on the railway, in a motor car, or on a bicycle or motorcycle enabled the consumption of a rural past. Eiluned and Peter Lewis, in their *The Land of Wales* (published in 1937), suggested that 'the traveller who buys a ticket at Paddington or Euston should be warned that he is about to travel backwards as well as westwards, for Wales is a storehouse of the past'.[41] Cycle tourists, as much as later motor-car tourists, were able to consume a version of the past by visiting castles, hearing Welsh being spoken and used as a living

A packed grandstand awaits the start of a cycle race at Carmarthen Park. Photographed by J.F. Lloyd at the beginning of the twentieth century, this image captures the excitement and anticipation before the starter's pistol fired. No helmets in those days!

One of the finest *vélodromes* ever built in Wales, Carmarthen Park and its cycling track opened in 1900. This photograph, taken by local photographer J.F. Lloyd, shows the park just before its grand unveiling on Easter Monday (16 April) that year. The bandstand and the park benches are all oriented towards the track itself. Carmarthen's new religion had arrived.

language, and escaping from facets of modern life such as electric lighting and urban noise.

Not all cycling, of course, was for touring purposes. Racing developed separately with its own national union — the National Cyclists' Union (NCU) — and separate clubs dedicated to track cycling. Historic examples include the Cardiff Racing Club, formed in 1893 which was based at the Three Horse Shoes on the High Street in the centre of the city. Membership of this club was set at 2s 6d — the equivalent of a single workmen's ticket to watch a rugby game at the Arms Park.[42] Originally, cycle racing had taken place on the streets but in 1890 the NCU banned its members from using the streets for all racing except time trialling. This ran in advance of the law, which was changed in 1896 to make cycle racing on the streets illegal, and, as a consequence, in place of the public highway came cycling tracks.

The built heritage of cycle racing is difficult to trace in modern towns and cities since many of the tracks that were built in the late-nineteenth century and early-twentieth centuries existed only for a short period before being put to use for other sports — typically soccer or rugby. The most accessible today is the great concrete track at Carmarthen Park, which opened in 1900. The design, with its long straights, banked corners and rugby pitch at the centre, was partly based on the tracks which then existed at Villa Park in Birmingham and at Crystal Palace in London.

Historians have not always been kind in their assessment of the tracks that were built. In his classic study of sport in Glamorgan, for example, Gareth Williams observes that most of the cycling tracks were 'ramshackle'.[43] Merthyr's cycling track, situated at Penydarren Park certainly fitted into this category. 'The track', complained the *Western Mail*'s correspondent 'is absolutely dangerous to ride upon'. Its three corners were sharp and on one side there was little protection from a six-foot drop.[44] Few, though, were quite so bad, even if equally few could compare with the great French *vélodromes* of the period.

At the start of the twentieth century, most major towns in Wales had at least one track. They were constructed in one of three ways — by a private company with the support of local cycling clubs, by the clubs themselves, or by the local authority — and varied in size and fitness for purpose. Sophia Gardens had a track from the mid-1880s and the Harlequins Ground on Newport Road provided an alternative, commercial venue for cycle racing into the twentieth century.[45] The commonest approach to cycling tracks taken by local authorities was to situate them within multi-purpose sports facilities. The original cycling track at Swansea, laid out at the St Helen's ground by the corporation in the mid-1880s, was squeezed between the rugby and cricket pitches and was markedly the junior sport at the site.[46] Despite support from the Swansea Harriers Cycling and Athletics Club, eventually they got fed up and sought their own independent track. This was built on the Vetch Field in 1897.[47] The triangular track, constrained by the unusual shape of the Vetch in its pre-football days, was something of a financial disaster, creditors going bankrupt as a result.[48]

A similar relationship between team sports and cycling prevailed at Llanelli. Originally based at the People's Park in the town centre, in 1894, the Llanelli Wheelers' Cycling Club joined in with two businessmen to construct a cycling track two miles away near the Halfway Hotel, Pemberton. Intending to lay out a football pitch in addition to the track, the syndicate were warned by their architect that if an effective, four laps to the mile facility were to be constructed, then the football project would have to be abandoned. Although a pitch was laid out in the centre of the track, it would not be until 1912, when Llanelli AFC made it their home, that a top-flight side would play there. Costing £300 to construct and with a capacity for 10,000 spectators, the ground opened on 12 April 1895.[49] The pitch was put to use by Halfway RFC, which formed in 1903, and the Halfway Quoits Club set up the following year. The County Athletics Grounds (as the site was known) remained in use by the soccer club until 1922 when it moved to Stebonheath and subsequently became a venue for boxing before falling into disrepair by the late-1930s. The location now forms part of the Parc-y-Scarlets complex.

Taff Vale Park, in Pontypridd, which had been laid out in the 1890s by the town's rugby club, became in the Edwardian period a venue catering for a wide variety of sporting activity from foot and pedestrian racing and athletics events to some of the major cycling events in the south Wales valleys. Featuring a banked track with two long straights, Taff Vale Park was a popular venue with cyclists in the area. Historians of cycling have often observed that racing developed in Britain following innovations in France and the United States. Unsurprisingly, the Linton brothers and Jimmy Michael (and others) regularly raced at the *vélodromes* of Paris and other French cities where their exploits earned them fame, admirers, and aspiring apprentices on the tracks of Pontypridd, Aberaman, and elsewhere.[50]

In the economic depression of the 1920s and 1930s, the bicycle offered an escape from the day-to-day routine of unemployment or the regularity of work underground for young men such as the novelist Ron Berry. In his autobiography, *History is What You Live*, Berry describes his experiences of cycling out of Rhondda in the late 1930s. Encouraged by his mate Vernon Rees, Berry joined the Clarion Cycle Club in Pentre though he eschewed club meets since 'it was awkward trying to be just sociable cyclists'. Berry's Rhondda offered three routes of escape: the mountain road to Rhigos, the mountain road to Nantymoel, or the relatively flat run down to Pontypridd. 'We favoured the mountain roads', he explains, 'Two coal face lads scruffed into mining, our tap roots starving in the rubble of *laissez faire* economics, so we fell for romantic gripe'.[51] For those without a bicycle, walking offered a similar escape.[52]

But even as Berry and his friends roamed around the south Wales countryside, the age of the bicycle was beginning to wane.

With professional cyclists drawn from across Britain and Europe, cycle races at Taff Vale Park were popular events in the sporting calendar of Pontypridd. This photograph shows a busy stadium in 1908. The wooden boarding at the top of the bank was designed to block the view of those hoping to watch for free from the hillside opposite.

Increasing numbers of cars in British society from the 1920s onwards has altered the relationship between tourism and the bicycle and the tensions between motorists and cyclists, so common in the pages of twenty-first century newspapers, have their origins in this period.[53] Prior to the 1940s, the commute to work took place either on foot, on bicycle, or via public transport but by the 1960s most men travelled to work in a car. This would not be the case for women until the 1980s.[54]

The perceived dominance of the car for tourism was noted in the reconstruction plans written during the latter stages of the Second World War. The A470, which winds its way through the heart of Wales, was designed to bring much needed holiday traffic into poor rural areas of the country in an effort to ensure that money earned in industrial Wales would be spent as far as possible in rural or 'holiday Wales'.[55] In a similar way, local councils, such as Barry Corporation, considered it important to provide a car park in their public parks to meet projected demand from tourists and local residents alike. One of the consequences of the growing dominance of the car in post-war Britain was the 'rediscovery' by walkers and cyclists of more neglected country roads. This was a process that had begun in the late 1920s. As Reginald Wellbye, writing in the CTC's guidebook of routes for the West Midlands and Wales (published in 1931), observed:

There is to be noticed the enormous increase in the number of motor vehicles on the roads, a circumstance which forces itself as much upon the attention of the wheelmen whose wanderings are confined to week-ends – when there is little or no commercial traffic – as upon those who may be on the road at other times. This, naturally, has had the effect of making the pleasure cyclist considerably more interested in by-way routes even than he was before.[56]

Overcoming the clash between motor vehicles, cyclists, and walkers gave rise, in the last quarter of the twentieth century, to dedicated routes for those using bicycles. The National Cycle Network (NCN), which has been developed since the mid-1980s by Sustrans in partnership with local authorities, now links the four corners of Wales together. The premier route: *Lôn Las Cymru* (NCN 8) runs from Cardiff through to Holyhead. For much of its route it coincides with the Taff Trail, a popular 55-mile walking and cycling route from Cardiff to Brecon, which was opened in 1988. Whilst promotion of green modes of transport has seen the bicycle rehabilitated to city and town centres with cycle routes being laid out to encourage less use of the car for commuting to work, it is cycle tourism that has stayed the course even though, in twenty-first-century Britain, we are more likely to drive with the bicycle to the pretty parts of the countryside rather than cycle all the way there.

The popularity of the bicycle and cycling and later the car and rallying and the *grand prix* has broadly overshadowed the motorcycle and motorcycling. Yet, for many young, working-class men in the inter-war years and beyond, the motorcycle was a thrilling and above all fast means of travelling around. The motorcycle had grown in importance during the Great War when they were regularly used for dispatches and communication between headquarters and the front lines.[57] Improvements in reliability and speed, as well as better mass-manufacturing methods, ensured that in the post-war period a motorcycle could be bought much more cheaply than before 1914. Advocates came from a wide variety of backgrounds and the desirability of being more mobile than in previous generations was increasingly within the grasp of working-class people. For many, the sheer thrill of travelling at high speed was a sufficient reason to desire a motorcycle; for some, though, it had other purposes. In the midst of the miners' lockout of 1926, the *Daily Mail* opined: 'Give a man a motorcycle to ride and to tend in his spare time and you take him from one of the chief causes of disgruntlement'.[58]

Competitive motorcycling in the inter-war years comprised of two particular forms: hill climbs and time trials and the

By the early part of the twentieth century, the bicycle was being replaced by the motorcycle as a means of travelling into and touring the countryside. This photograph shows Ferndale Motorcycle Club in 1909.

Motorcyclists also took to racing, as this photograph taken at Carmarthen Park by J.F. Lloyd illustrates. Speed, noise, and the smell of oil brought men and women, young and old to the track to experience its thrills.

commercialised spectacle of speedway. Hill climbs and time trials provided the mainstay of activity for many local motorcycle clubs.[59] In Cardiff, these took place heading out of the city from Thornhill on Caerphilly Mountain. In Swansea, the local motorcycle club held its first race on Fairy Hill on the Gower in 1924 and similar hill climbs could be found in Aberdare, Pontypridd, Merthyr and the Rhondda.[60] With the advent of speedway in the late-1920s, more formal race tracks were established and these became the mainstay of competitive motorcycling by the 1960s with Llandow circuit near Cardiff being one of the most popular before the establishment of the Pembrey circuit in Carmarthenshire in the 1980s.

The number of motorcycling clubs grew steadily in the 1920s. When the process of forming an East South Wales centre of the Auto Cycle Union (ACU) began in January 1921, it was attended by four clubs: Cardiff, Newport, Bargoed and Tredegar. The minutes also mention the existence of Aberdare and Blaenavon Motorcycle Clubs. By the time of the annual meeting of the centre in December of that year, eight clubs were recognised with Abergavenny, Blaina, Brynmawr and Cwmbran added.[61] By the early 1930s, the number of members had expanded to thirteen and included Pontypridd, Barry and Merthyr Tydfil amongst others; there were a further five clubs in south west Wales. A separate centre existed for north Wales.[62]

This series of remarkable images taken in the 1920s capture the zany character of hill trialling: a time-trial sport that was particularly popular on Caerphilly Mountain. Note the laid-back sidecar passenger smoking his cigarette and the distressed female passenger who dare not look!

The heyday of motorcycle racing came after the Second World War with the resurgence of speedway in the 1950s and the growth of circuit racing across Britain. In Wales, these developments were registered in the form of new speedway stadiums in Cardiff and Newport but also in more unlikely venues such as Aberdare Park and Neath Abbey. Since 1952, the racing circuit at Aberdare Park has hosted designated national races attracting leading stars of motorcycle racing such as Mike Hailwood and Carl Fogarty. In later years, races would be held at Cyfarthfa Park in Merthyr. Both replaced the earlier presence of speedway and provided an avenue for new fans and local supporters to enjoy a sport which was otherwise only broadcast from major circuits in England and around the world. Not unsurprisingly, the landscape of Wales has continued to attract motorcyclists just as it continues to attract walkers, mountaineers, and cyclists. Popular routes through the Brecon Beacons on the A470 or the Black Mountain in Carmarthenshire remain at the heart of motorcycle touring and in more recent years motocross has brought young motorcyclists into smaller communities such as Ynysybwl and Builth Wells where racing and practice circuits have been laid out.

Into the Caves, Onto the Rivers

The use of the natural landscape for sporting and recreational activity has consistently evolved over the course of the twentieth century. Today, the hills and mountains, caves and rivers are the backdrop and location of a diverse range of leisure from canoeing and potholing to diving and fell running. Although these have never reached the heights of the cycling craze of the 1890s or the motorcycling craze of the inter-war years, they nevertheless represent the steady expansion of countryside as a playground for everyone. This has not always been met with open access: kayakers in particular suffer from inadequate access agreements meaning that paddling on rivers in many parts of Wales is still considered trespass and liable to civil action by landowners.

Kayaking and canoeing arrived in Britain from North America in the nineteenth century but it was not until the 1960s that the thrill and challenge of navigating tumbling rapids grew into a popular sport. Advances in technology, especially fibreglass boats and later plastic ones, which made more complex and tailor-made designs possible, have expanded the possibilities of kayaking. Canoe polo, free-styling events involving using a kayaker's skill to pull tricks akin to those of BMX bikers and skateboarders, marathon canoeing and slalom racing have all developed over the course of the twentieth century. Although most kayaking takes place on rivers and, for practice purposes, in heated indoor swimming pools, Wales is also home to the Tryweryn White Water Centre near Bala, which has been one of the major centres for the sport since the 1980s. A second, artificial centre, opened in March 2010 at the International Sports Village in Cardiff Bay and provides facilities for white water and slalom runs similar to those available at the National Water Sports Centre in Nottingham.

Caving, in contrast to kayaking, has been practised in Wales since the eighteenth century. Initial interest in caves came from scientific exploration rather than leisure and it was not until the early part of the twentieth century that caving and potholing grew

An essential part of regional legend, cross country running has been popular for centuries and athletes such as Guto Nyth Bran continue to provide inspiration. This photograph of two runners was taken in fields near Ynysybwl just before the Great War.

as forms of recreation. The navigation of Dan-yr-Ogof in the Neath Valley (today's showcaves) by the Morgan brothers in 1912 and the opening up of the caves to greater numbers of potholers in the 1930s marked the beginnings of modern subterranean exploration as sport. Dan-yr-Ogof was opened as a show cave in August 1939 and remained open, despite war conditions, until 1941 when it was closed for over twenty years. Finally reopening in 1964, the cave complex at Dan-yr-Ogof is now one of the major tourist attractions in Britain — within just two years of opening, the Dan-yr-Ogof complex was attracting over 80,000 visitors and this remains the case today.

In the years between the closure of the showcave and its reopening, caving and potholing took root in earnest and several clubs were formed in the 1950s and 1960s including university clubs and those attached to schools such as Aberystwyth University and Brynmawr Caving Club. The earliest was the South Wales Caving Club, which formed in 1946 and is one of the largest caving clubs in Britain. A surge in the popularity of caving came after the discoveries at Dan-yr-Ogof in the spring of 1966. A group of six potholers led by Alan Coase of the south Wales club uncovered a large complex of caves and passages which extended the Morgan brothers' findings by over a mile and a half. The story — and photographs taken by Coase — was published in *The Observer* a few months later and brought fresh attention.[63]

Kayaking and caving are modern sports that require a degree of specialist equipment and specialist knowledge. In contrast, running, whether cross country, marathon or road racing, is a far older sport and exists in the mythology of several parts of Wales.[64] In the cemetery at St Gwynno's Church near Pontypridd stands the grave of one such mythological runner: Guto Nyth Bran. His feats are remembered each year in the Nos Galan road race with a celebrity runner leading the race through Mountain Ash in the Cynon valley. The Nos Galan races began in 1958 and have been run, albeit with a break between 1973 and 1984, ever since. The Nyth Bran legend is well-known throughout the south Wales valleys and tells the story of Gruffydd Morgan (1700-1737). Born in Llwyncelyn near Porth in the Rhondda, Morgan's running prowess first came to the attention of his compatriots when helping his father on the family farm.[65] According to the legend Guto won many races and retired successfully before the age of 30. Settled down with his former manager and wife *Siân o'r Siop*, Guto was persuaded out of retirement in 1837 to race against a mysterious English opponent known simply as Prince.

The race extended over 12 miles between Newport and the church in Bedwas near Caerphilly. Prince took an early lead and the race appeared lost until an uphill surge by Guto took him past his opponent and on to victory. Glanffrwd recounts that the 12 miles were covered by Guto in just 53 minutes. Tired and exhausted from the race, Guto was greeted by his wife Siân who proceeded to slap him on the back in congratulation. The slap however proved fatal and, with the last wind knocked out of him, Guto died in Siân's arms. His body was interred at St Gwynno's church in Llanwynno

Athletics meets, held every year near summer bank holidays, drew large crowds to watch the exploits of the runners and cyclists. Taken by J. F. Lloyd in the early years of the twentieth century, this photograph of Carmarthen Park shows just how large those crowds could be.

and it is here that each New Year's Eve a service of remembrance is held to mark Guto Nyth Bran's achievements.

In the nineteenth century, running came to be formalised just like many other sports and often took place alongside cycling events at athletics tournaments held at stadiums and in public parks throughout the country. In the twentieth century, running developed along two parallel courses — track racing and cross country. At Taff Vale Park in Pontypridd, powderhall sprint races were run from the first decade of the century and remained a prominent part of the venue's sporting activities until the late-1920s. These races drew international participants and were famous across Britain. Not long after powderhall racing began at Taff Vale Park, the organisers of the International Cross Country Championships (ICCC) agreed that the 1906 competition should be hosted at the racecourse in Caerleon. The ICCC had begun in 1903 as a contest between the four home nations before being expanded to include continental European competitors from 1907. Wales hosted the ICCC on eight occasions prior to their transfer to the International Amateur Athletics Federation in 1973. Six of those championships were held at Caerleon and two at Cardiff. Since the Second World War, cross country and fell running have grown in size and popularity with many of the prominent races that now take place dating from the 1970s and 1980s.

The countryside has long been a central part of the recreational landscape. Though its boundaries were rarely formalised until after the Second World War, the countryside exists as the once and future playground of everyone: prior to industrialisation almost all recreational activity took place within its environs with only small numbers of fields dedicated to sports such as handball and bando. Today, though use of the dedicated sporting environment far exceeds the use of the countryside, the surge in popularity of running, kayaking, cycling, walking and climbing has brought new people out of towns and cities and into the rural landscape where youth hostels, clubs bunkhouses and hotels and guesthouses cater for the needs of tourists. High in the hills and mountains or paddling on the rivers and waterways, Wales has become a national park.

Splashing about in local streams has long been part of childhood adventure, as this photograph of young children taken near Roath Park in about 1900 shows. It reflects the importance of the entire landscape as a place of play.

Conclusion

We're all of us human beings. High and low we come from the same place, we survive somehow and then we fade away.

Ron Berry, *So Long, Hector Bebb* (1970).

The variety of Wales' sporting heritage is remarkable and tells us much about the nation's rich past. From staples such as public parks and stadiums to welfare grounds and open-air swimming baths built by unemployed volunteers, there is much to be cherished and much still to be recorded and championed. Since the emergence of modern sport in the nineteenth century, the landscape of towns and cities and villages in the countryside has been altered by the needs of players and spectators and as sport continues to evolve so too do the facilities in which it is played. Evolution and change is, then, at the heart of what sport and sporting heritage is all about. To gaze at the turf at the centre of the Millennium Stadium is not to look upon the hallowed ground of the Arms Park whereupon stars of decades past from Frank Hancock and Arthur Gould to JPR Williams and Gareth Edwards thrilled captivated audiences, but it is to look upon a place that has been used continuously for sport for much of the last two hundred years.

A rugby field, a public park, bowling green or soccer stadium are all essential elements of Wales' industrial past and important facets of its future. As a form of civic space they are as relevant to the study of modern society as chapels and cinemas, miners' institutes and railway stations, and country houses and town halls.[1] They are equally of interest to a great many people who are not otherwise animated by more traditional aspects of industrial or pre-industrial architecture and heritage. Sporting places have become key features of community identity, of

Advertising boards for entry to the Arms Park greyhound track alongside parked bicycles, cars, and pedestrians, as they appeared in the early 1930s. This image captures the diversity of Wales' sporting heritage from the great stadiums of top-flight sport to the roads used by children for a kick-about and the bicycles and cars used to escape in to the countryside.

national identity and of individual identity: the site where a child scores their first goal or try, the ground where a local side wins the league championship or cup, the stadium where Wales wins the Grand Slam or (one day perhaps) wins the World Cup. It may even be argued that 'sport is one of the reasons why a strong sense of Welshness has survived'.[2]

This book has drawn on material gathered together by the Royal Commission on the Ancient and Historical Monuments of Wales over the last four years on the sporting heritage and sporting landscapes of Wales. In keeping with the surveys undertaken on individual cities by English Heritage (on Manchester) in the early 2000s and more recently by Historic Scotland (on Glasgow) and the Played in Britain team led by Simon Inglis (on Tyne and Wear, Birmingham, Liverpool and London), it has shown the variety of Welsh sporting places and the strong connections they have to the other great stories of the history of Wales. A great deal of what was built nearly a century ago continues to form both the basis of everyday recreation and the lower levels of sporting competition. Cricketers at Lymore Park in Montgomery play on the same ground as their ancestors of the 1840s, golfers at Ynyslas enjoy an unbroken lineage stretching back to the 1880s and junior rugby players at Taff Vale Park in Pontypridd play on ground first used for the fifteen-man game in 1890. The appearance of these grounds has changed in the sense that pavilions and stands have been refurbished, rebuilt or demolished but the essential characteristics of the ground as a sporting place remain the same.

In recording these sites, the Royal Commission is fortunate to be able to draw upon remarkable collections of aerial photography taken variously by private companies such as Aerofilms and by state bodies including the RAF and the Commission itself. Some of these images date from the earliest

Taken by Aerofilms in 1921, this photograph of Swansea's St Helen's rugby and cricket ground captured the great variety of sporting passions in the town: rugby matches alongside soccer ones, tennis alongside bowls, scratch games alongside scheduled ones. Yet, this scene could not be reproduced today: the tennis courts no longer exist and much of the playing field below is now a car park.

days of aerial reconnaissance and place into the historical record fascinating snapshots of a nation at play. In this book we have seen the crowded bob banks of the Vetch in 1921, the playing of tennis amidst the ruins of the Bishop's Palace in St David's and families basking in the sunshine on the grass of Ynysangharad Park in

Pontypridd. It is also possible to view the processes of change over time. This is particularly true of more famous venues such as the Arms Park that were photographed regularly: new stands, demolished pavilions, the laying out of running tracks, and even the worn-out grass at the end of the season all stand out.

The Wales National Stadium as it was in the mid-1990s just prior to demolition. Open terraces, a relic of a former age, contrast with the double-tiered, all-seater stands and the pristine playing surface where the hopes and dreams of Wales were played out.

Under-appreciation, as well as necessary change, has sadly taken its toll. Open-air swimming baths that were built throughout the south Wales valleys and the north Wales coast in the 1920s and 1930s have been demolished as habits and expectations have shifted towards heated, indoor pools and the fun of water slides and wave machines. In times of austerity, too, finite budgets have been unable to meet the costs of running facilities that can only be open a few months of the year. Sports such as quoiting and greyhound racing have all but disappeared from the landscape and the facilities that once served them have gone as well. The weak financial position of many rugby and soccer clubs at the local level may well mean that grounds taken for granted today are lost in the future.

Celebrating our sporting heritage and conserving it by record or by statutory protection will ensure that its importance to modern society will not be forgotten. Just as we seek to preserve and understand the past through buildings, records and landscapes so too must we be careful to do so for our own time. Those fields of play that lie at the heart of every community are truly the core of Wales' sporting heritage.

Notes

Introduction: Up the Rec

1   B. L. Coombes, *These Poor Hands: The Autobiography of a Miner Working in South Wales* (London, 1939).
2   Gwyn Jones, *Times Like These* (London, 1936).
3   Welsh Reconstruction Advisory Council, *First Interim Report* (London, 1944).
4   Hazel Conway, *People's Parks: The Design and Development of Victorian Parks in Britain* (Cambridge, 1991).
5   Louise Miskell, 'Recreational Space in a Resort Town: Park versus Beach in Nineteenth-century Swansea', in *Transactions of the Honourable Society of Cymmrodorion*, n.s. 15 (2009), 87–104. Earlier considerations of the theme in the Swansea context include: J. Alun Owen, *Swansea's Earliest Open Spaces* (Swansea, 1995); Tom Ridd, 'Swansea's Parks and Public Libraries', *Glamorgan Historian*, 6 (1969); Tom Ridd, 'Thomas y Lân: The Welsh Pioneer of Open Spaces', *Gower*, 15 (1962).
6   Richard Hoggart, *The Uses of Literacy: Aspects of Working-class Life* (London, [1957] 2009), 298.
7   Conway, *People's Parks*. Eadem, *Public Parks* (Oxford, 1996).
8   Roy Rosenzweig, 'The Parks and the People: Social History and Urban Parks', *Journal of Social History*, 18 (1984), 290.
9   Roy Rosenzweig, *Eight Hours For What We Will: Workers and Leisure in an Industrial City, 1870–1920* (Cambridge, 1983), 127–8.
10 Tony Wilmott, *The Roman Amphitheatre in Britain* (Stroud, 2008).
11 Mary Beard, *Pompeii* (London, 2008), 259–260.
12 *Merthyr Guardian*, 27 September 1834.
13 Glanffrwd, *Llanwynno,* (Cardiff, [1888] 1949), 68–76.
14 Gareth Williams, 'Sport and Society in Glamorgan, 1780–1980', 111–15, in idem, *1905 and All That: Essays on Rugby Football, Sport and Welsh Society* (Llandysul, 1991). See also: 'Popular Culture, Leisure and Recreation', in Chris Williams and Sian Rhiannon Williams (eds), *Gwent County History, Volume 4: Industrial Monmouthshire, 1780–1914* (Cardiff, 2011).
15 Prys Morgan, 'From a Death to a View: The Hunt for the Welsh Past in the Romantic Period', in Eric Hobsbawm and Terence Ranger (eds), *The Invention of Tradition*, (Cambridge, 1983), 54.
16 *Western Mail*, 6 October 1891.
17 Alan Metcalfe, 'Organized Sport in the Mining Communities of South Northumberland, 1800-1889', *Victorian Studies* 25 (1982), 491.

Invented in the United States in 1891 by James Naismith, basketball has had a long association with the YMCA and other proponents of sport that is free from the effects of professionalisation, gambling and alcohol. The sport arrived in Britain shortly after its invention. By the inter-war years, it was widespread and played especially at YMCA and Boys' Club halls around the country. This photograph of a match was taken at Aberaman YMCA in the Cynon Valley.

Chapter I: The Public Park

1   *Cardiff and Merthyr Guardian*, 7 March 1857.
2   'Letter from Alexander Roos to Onesiphorus Tyndall Bruce', 15 August 1851, *National Archives of Scotland*: Hamilton Bruce Papers, Bute Estate Correspondence – GD152/198/18/1. The bowling green was a nod to the Scottish roots of the Butes.
3   *Report of the Commissioners ... [on] Boundaries and Wards ... of Boroughs and Corporate Towns* (London: House of Commons, 1837), Part I, 261, 21; Part II, 347, 311; Part III, 251.
4   *Cardiff and Merthyr Guardian*, 12 June 1858.
5   *Bristol Mercury*, 5 June 1858.
6   Cardiff Local Board of Health, *Minute Books*, 2 July 1858 [Glamorgan Record Office: BC/LB].
7   Parliamentary Papers, 'Report from the Select Committee on Public Walks', (London, 1833), 8.
8   As above.
9   *Western Mail*, 24 September 1898.
10 Louise Miskell, *'Intelligent Town': An Urban History of Swansea, 1780–1855* (Cardiff, 2006).
11 Colonel George Grant Francis, *On the 'St Helen's' and other Sites for a Public Park at Swansea* (Swansea, 1878), 4.
12 *Western Mail*, 12 May 1870.
13 Borough of Swansea Waters and Sewers Committee, *Minutes*, 23 September 1853 [West Glamorgan Record Office: TC1/2].
14 As above, 20 May 1869.
15 *Cambrian*, 18 August 1871.
16 *Cambrian*, 25 August 1871.
17 *Penny Illustrated*, 16 November 1889.
18 *Cambrian*, 2 October 1874.
19 *Swansea Journal*, 24 October 1874.
20 Borough of Swansea, *Minute Book, 1882–1888*, 13 May, 10 June 1885; Borough of Swansea: Parks & Open Spaces Committee, *Minute Book, 1887–1904*, 8 February 1887.
21 As above, 18 September 1889.
22 *Western Mail*, 20 May 1880.
23 *Western Mail*, 19 September 1899.
24 *Cardiff and Suburban News*, 15 November 1924.
25 *Cardiff and Suburban News*, 28 February 1924.
26 *Western Mail*, 15 December 1887, 28 January, 8 February, 21 February, 24 May 1888.
27 *Western Mail*, 14 March 1893.
28 *Western Mail*, 6 July 1894.
29 *Western Mail*, 11 September 1894.
30 *Western Mail*, 20 March, 11 April 1899.
31 *Western Mail*, 10 September 1894.
32 Waymark, *Thomas Mawson*, 191.
33 *Western Mail*, 17 June 1897.

34 *Gardeners' Chronicle*, 7 July 1894.

35 *Wrexham Advertiser*, 1 July 1871. One resident of Wrexham complained: 'Look at Llangollen and Oswestry, to see how they beat us'.

36 Edmund Stonelake (ed. Antony Mor O'Brien), *The Autobiography of Edmund Stonelake* (Bridgend, 1981), 56.

37 As above, 39.

38 *The Times*, 3 March 1932.

39 E. E. Edwards, *Echoes of Rhymney* (Risca, 1974). The park was officially opened on 9 May 1925. Efforts were made to lay out a recreation ground in Pontlottyn in the mid-1890s and came to fruition in the early 1900s. *Western Mail*, 20 March 1893.

40 *Western Mail*, 22 October 1874.

41 *Western Mail*, 16 June 1881.

42 *Western Mail*, 18 August 1881.

43 *Western Mail*, 17 August 1882.

44 *Merthyr Express*, 26 February 1887.

45 *Merthyr Express*, 12 February 1887.

46 *Merthyr Express*, 16 January 1897.

47 Merthyr Tydfil Urban District Council, *Incorporation of Merthyr Tydfil: Statistical Information* (Merthyr Tydfil, 1903), 23.

48 Harold Carter and Sandra Wheatley, *Merthyr Tydfil in 1851: A Study in the Spatial Structure of a Welsh Industrial Town* (Cardiff, 1982), 34.

49 *Western Mail*, 10 July 1869.

50 *Western Mail*, 5 September 1900. The ground was originally known as the barn field and was purchased by the local council in 1898. Transformed into Abertillery Park and Recreation Ground, it had been the home of the local rugby club since 1895.

51 A flavour of these articles, as well as Pettigrew's vision of municipal parks, can be found in his *Municipal Parks: Layout, Management and Administration* (London, 1937).

52 *Gardeners' Chronicle*, 12 January, 6 July, 26 January, 2 February 1907.

53 Borough of Swansea, Parks Committee, *Minutes of Meetings, 1904–1911*, 3 October 1905, 2 October 1906, 5 May, 1 September, 6 October 1908; Borough of Swansea, Parks Committee, *Minutes of Meetings, 1911–1913*, 24 September 1912; Borough of Swansea, Parks Committee, *Minutes of Meetings, 1913–1917*, 12 December 1916.

54 *Aberdare Times*, 12 June 1869.

55 *Western Mail*, 23 August 1871.

56 *Western Mail*, 19 March, 20 August 1890.

57 *Rhondda Socialist*, 3 August 1912.

58 André Berry, 'Wrexham's Urban Parks, Part I: Bellevue (The Parciau)', *Transactions of the Denbighshire Historical Society*, 47 (1997), 103–136.

59 *Merthyr Pioneer*, 15 April 1911.

60 Gwyn A. Williams, *When Was Wales: A History of the Welsh* (London, 1985), 258.

61 Pontardawe Rural District Council, *Annual Report of the Medical Officer of Health* (Pontardawe, 1933), 17.

62 *History of Cwmparc: King Coal Invades the Sylvan Valley – Awarded the Prize at the Treorchy Semi-National Eisteddfod in 1923* (Pontypridd, 1936), 33. *Western Mail*, 19 June 1889, 2 December 1890.

63 Eli Taylor, 'Report on Existing Facilities for Recreation, 9 December 1937', Rhondda Urban District Council, Surveyor's Department, *Surveyor's Reports, 1937*. The list does not include the miners' welfare facilities throughout Rhondda.

64 Eli Taylor, 'Report on Playing Fields, 18 October 1930', Rhondda Urban District Council, Surveyor's Department, *Surveyor's Reports, 1930*.

65 *Merthyr Pioneer*, 15 April 1911.

66 Swansea Corporation, Unemployment Committee, *Minutes of Meetings*, 12 July 1922, 11 January 1926.

67 *Second Report of the Commissioner for the Special Areas*, Cmd. 5090 (London, 1935), 72.

68 *Third Report of the Commissioner for the Special Areas*, Cmd. 5303 (London, 1935–6), xii, 131.

69 Rhondda Urban District Council, Surveyor's Department, 'Gelligaled Costings, 19 June 1925' [Glamorgan Archives: D276/3/12].

70 Eli Taylor, 'Uncirculated Report on Playing Field Schemes, 6 May 1930', Rhondda Urban District Council, Surveyor's Department, *Surveyor's Reports, 1930*.

71 Eli Taylor, 'Report on Playing Fields, 18 October 1930'.

72 Eli Taylor, 'Report to Members of the Health Committee, 18 September 1931', Rhondda Urban District Council, Surveyor's Department, *Surveyor's Reports, 1931*.

73 Richard Holt, *Sport and the British: A Modern History* (Oxford, 1990), 271.

74 *Journal of the National Playing Fields Association*, 1 (1931), 30. There was also a county branch in Anglesey founded in 1930.

75 *Glamorgan Free Press and Rhondda Leader*, 4 June 1927.

76 *Journal of the National Playing Fields Association*, 1 (1930), 24. Eighteen were situated in Glamorgan and ten in Monmouthshire.

77 *Journal of the National Playing Fields Association*, 2 (1933), 98–99.

78 Glamorgan Playing Fields Association, *Annual Report for 1929*. Glamorgan Archives: DPL/996.

79 Miners' welfare is discussed in chapter 3.

80 Letter from W. H. L. Chattin to Captain F. Johnson, October 10 1930', Glamorgan Archives: DPL/996.

81 W. H. L. Chattin, 'Draft Annual Report for 1933', Glamorgan Archives: DPL/996.

82 Trades Union Congress, *Report of the Annual Trades Union Congress: Newcastle, 1932* (London, 1932), 260.

83 *Sports Facilities in Wales: A Survey by the Central Council of Physical Recreation (Wales)* (Cardiff, 1963), 10.

84 County Borough of Swansea, *Development Plan* (Swansea, 1955), 97.

85 *Labour Party Bulletin*, 4 (October 1945), 111.

86 *Cardiff and Suburban News*, 21 February 1948.

87 CCPR Report, 51.

88 Arvid Bengtsson (ed.), *Adventure Playgrounds* (New York, 1972); Jack Lambert & Jenny Pearson, *Adventure Playgrounds: A Personal Account of a Play-Leader's Work* (London, 1974).

Chapter II: Swimming Pools

1 *Llantrisant Observer*, 27 July, 2 November 1957. The baths lay a quarter of a mile upstream from the town centre.

2 By 2010, there were 142 swimming pools in Wales. I am grateful to John Hinton of Sport Wales for this figure.

3 *Western Mail*, 2 May 1958.

4 *North Wales Chronicle*, 23 June 1900.

5 *Wrexham Advertiser*, 4 April 1874.

6 *Denbighshire Advertiser*, 19 June 1858.

7 *Denbighshire Advertiser*, 17 June 1854.

8 *Denbighshire Advertiser*, 12 June 1858.

9 *Denbighshire Advertiser*, 4 July 1857.

10 *Glamorgan Free Press*, 13 July 1895.

11 *South Wales Daily News*, 2 July, 16 July 1912.

12 *Cambrian Daily Leader*, 30 September 1897.

13 *South Wales Echo*, 30 April 1896.

14 *Western Mail*, 23 May 1899.

15 Agnes Campbell, *Report on Public Baths and Wash-houses in the United Kingdom* (Edinburgh, 1918), 7–8.

16 *Aberdare Leader*, 20 April 1934.

17 Thomas Blight, *In Living Memory* (Milton Keynes, 2007), 7; Ann Eyles & Con O'Sullivan, *In the Shadow of the Steelworks: Reminiscences of a Splott Childhood in the 1930s* (Cardiff, 1992), 2; Radyr & Morganstown New Horizons History Group, *Memories of Radyr and Morganstown* (Radyr, 1993), 68.

18 Burry Port Urban District Council, *Medical Officer of Health Annual Report 1936* (Burry Port, 1936).

19 Walter Haydn Davies, *The Right Place, The Right Time* (Swansea, 1975 edn.), 158.

20 Gerald Edwards, 'Taffs Well Spa' in Pentyrch and District Local History Society, *The Garth Domain*, 15 (April 2002), 22.

21 *Glamorgan Free Press*, 20 August 1932.

22 Rhondda Urban District Council, Surveyor's Department, *Reports January–December 1930*, 7 May 1930.

23 Rhondda Urban District Council, *Minutes of Council*, 23 January 1934.

24 *Rhondda Vanguard*, December 1935, 3. The vote was 6–4 in favour of Treherbert with the Labour Party split by community loyalty.

25 *Aberdare Leader*, 15 June 1938.

26 Rhondda Urban District Council, Surveyor's Department, *Reports January 1934–December 1934*, 21 September 1934.

27 *Aberdare Leader*, 16 May 1935.

28 W. John Owen, *My Memories of Cilfynydd from the 1930s* (Pontypridd, 2011), 40.

29 Bala Urban District Council, *Medical Officer of Health Annual Report 1938* (Bala, 1938).

30 *Llantrisant Observer*, 16 February 1957.

31 *Llantrisant and Llantwit Fardre Rural District: Official Guide* (London, 1972).

32 W. Nelmes, 'Post-War Planning and Development: Report of Director of Parks', 1943, 14–15.

33 *Western Mail*, 2 May 1958.

34 Central Council for Physical Recreation (Wales), *Sports Facilities in Wales* (Cardiff, 1963).

35 *Cambrian News*, 9 August 1985.

36 *Daily Telegraph*, 29 February 2008.

37 *South Wales Echo*, 15 April 2009.

Chapter III: Welfare Grounds

1 John E. Morgan, *A Village Workers' Council and what it accomplished: Being a Short History of the Lady Windsor Lodge [SWMF]* (Pontypridd, 1950), 66.

2 Lady Windsor Lodge, *Minutes of Meetings 27 November 1903–28 April 1907*, 7 November, 5 December 1906.

3 Mountain Ash Urban District Council, *Minutes of Council, April 1910–September 1910*, 12 July 1910.

4 Mountain Ash Urban District Council, Surveyor's Department, *Reports September 1910–October 1914*, 9 May, 23 May 1911.

5 Lady Windsor Lodge, *Minutes of Meetings 1903–1907*, 2 January, 16 January 1907.

6 Morgan, *Village Workers' Council*, 66.

7 *Western Mail*, 29 April 1897.

8 'Abel Morgan Interview', South Wales Miners' Library: AUD/311.

9 *Western Mail*, 3 November 1916.

10 Mining Industry Act 1920, s.20 (1). This is available online: http://www.legislation.gov.uk/ukpga/Geo5/10-11/50/contents/enacted.

11 Miners' Welfare Fund, *Tenth Annual Report of the Miners' Welfare Commission* (London, 1939), 102.

12 *Ocean and National Magazine*, 2 (1929), 111.

13 Miners' Welfare Commission, *Seventeenth Annual Report* (London, 1939), 88.

14 Ministry of Health, *Report of the South Wales Regional Survey Committee* (London, 1921), 58.

15 *The Times*, 29 July 1922; *Glamorgan Free Press and Rhondda Leader*, 23 May 1924.

16 *Glamorgan Free Press and Rhondda Leader*, 10 May 1930.

17 Miners' Welfare Commission, *Seventeenth Annual Report*, 90.

18 Miners' Welfare Commission, *Sixth Annual Report* (London, 1928), 39.

19 *Industrial Welfare*, July 1925, 245.

20 Ocean Area Recreational Union, *Ten Years Later: A Report on Miners' Welfare Work in the South Wales Coalfield, 1921–1931* (Treorchy, 1931), 51–57.

21 *Industrial Welfare*, May 1926, 166–167; August 1926, 268; October 1926, 341; August 1927, 268.

22 Miners' Welfare Joint Committee for South Wales & Monmouthshire, *Minute Book No. 2*, 17 December 1930.

23 *Industrial Welfare*, June 1925, 213; *Industrial Welfare*, August 1927, 265; Miners' Welfare Joint Committee for South Wales & Monmouthshire, *Minute Book No. 2*, 17 December 1930.

24 *Caerphilly Journal*, 20 June 1931; Miners' Welfare Joint Committee for South Wales & Monmouthshire, *Minute Book No. 2*, 17 December 1930. The Senghenydd Project consisting of tennis courts, bowling greens, a recreation ground and pavilion had opened in 1925. *Industrial Welfare*, June 1925, 214.

25 Miners' Welfare Joint Committee for South Wales & Monmouthshire, *Minute Book No. 5*, 30 June 1947.

26 *South Wales Echo*, 28 December 1932.

27 'Letter from Blaenavon', in International Voluntary Service, *Report 1933–1934* (La Chaux-de-Fonds, 1934), 6–8.

28 International Voluntary Service, *Annual Report, 1934* (La Chaux-de-Fonds, 1934), 3.

29 This paragraph draws on Kitty Lewis' papers on the Rhos Camp. National Library of Wales: Kitty Idwal Jones Papers, files 28 and 30.

30 *Wrexham Leader*, 20 April 1932.

31 *Rhos Herald*, 2 July 1932.

32 *Rhos Herald*, 9 July 1932.

33 Kitty Lewis, 'An Adventure at Rhosllanerchrugog', *Welsh Outlook* (September 1932).

34 André Berry, 'Wrexham's Urban Parks II: Ponciau Banks', *Old Denbighshire: Transactions of the Denbighshire Historical Society*, 48 (1999).

35 G. M. Ll. Davies, 'To the Unemployed', *Cambrian News* (January 1935), 2.

36 David Gwyn, *Gwynedd: Inheriting a Revolution. The Archaeology of Industrialisation in North-West Wales* (Chichester, 2006), 206.

37 *Cardiff and Suburban News*, 19 November 1927.

38 *Ocean and National Magazine*, 2 (May 1929), 135.

39 *Cardiff and Suburban News*, 9 July, 20 August 1927, 23 June 1928. The wider history of David Morgan before 1919 can be traced in Brian Lee, *David Morgan Limited, The Family Store: An Illustrated History, 1879–2005* (Derby, 2005).

40 'Bridgend Urban District Council, Minutes of Surveyor's Department'. Glamorgan Archives: Edward Loveluck MSS, file 67 (D/DLOV).

41 The quotes are taken from Ian Michael Pincombe, 'Out of Rexville: G. F. Lovell and the South Wales Confectionery Industry, c. 1830 – c. 1940' (Unpublished PhD Thesis: University of Wales Cardiff, 1999), 246.

42 Johnes, *Soccer and Society*, 104.

43 Aberdare Valley Supports' Club Cricket League, *Handbook, 1949*, 5–6.

44 Cardiff and District (Wednesday) Baseball League, *Handbook, 1926*; *Handbook, 1928*.

45 Cardiff and District (Wednesday) Baseball League, *Handbook, 1929*.

46 Merthyr Tydfil Borough Police Athletic Club, *Minutes of Meetings*, 15 June 1921, 20 May 1936 [Glamorgan Archives: D/D CON/MT 11/5].

47 City of Cardiff Police, *Annual Report of the Chief Constable to the Watch Committee, 1937*, 16. At the turn of the century, it appears that patronage came from Lord Tredegar who allowed the Police to use the Harlequins Ground in Roath. *Police Chronicle*, 19 October 1901.

48 *North Wales Chronicle*, 4 July 1885.

49 *Western Mail*, 7 February 1885.

50 *Western Mail*, 11 October 1877.

51 *Western Mail*, 5 December 1882.

52 *Western Mail*, 8 September 1883.

53 *Western Mail*, 24 April 1900.

54 University College of Wales, *Calendar, 1884–1885*, 95; University College of Wales, *Calendar, 1887–1888*, 99.

55 *The University College of Wales Magazine*, November 1889, 63; Iwan Morgan (ed.), *The College by the Sea* (Aberystwyth, 1928), 303–06.

56 E. L. Ellis, *The University College of Wales, Aberystwyth, 1872–1972* (Cardiff, 1972), 161.

57 As above, 215.

58 University College of South Wales and Monmouthshire, *Students' Handbook: Session 1898–1899*, 39–46.

59 *North Wales Chronicle*, 16 October 1897.

60 Carol Dyhouse, *No Distinction of Sex? Women in British Universities, 1870–1939* (London, 1995), 206.

61 S.B. Chrimes, 'University College, Cardiff: A Centenary History, 1883–1983' (Unpublished), 94, 442.

62 University College of South Wales and Monmouthshire, Registrar's Files, 'Interview Notes dated 19 April 1928; 27 October 1928'.

63 Chrimes, 'University College', 450.

64 *Cap and Gown: The Magazine of the University College of South Wales and Monmouthshire*, 27 (June 1930), 32.

Chapter IV: Sporting Places

1 Dai Smith, 'Focal Heroes', in his *Aneurin Bevan and the World of South Wales* (Cardiff, 1993), 318–337.

2 *Rhondda Leader*, 4 September 1897.

3 George M. Evans, *A Bagful of Monkeys* (Llanrwst, 2004), 25; for Pontypridd see: Pontypridd & District Hospital Boxing Tournament Committee, *Souvenir Programme of the Boxing Tournament, April 18th 1932*.

4 Evans, *A Bagful...*, 35–36.

5 Eddie Thomas' gym was located in the former Billiard Hall in Penydarren.

6 R. J. Moore-Colyer, 'Gentlemen, Horses and the Turf in Nineteenth-Century Wales', *Welsh History Review*, 16 (1992), 49.

7 *Bell's Life in London and Sporting Chronicle*, 9 February 1878.

8 *Bell's Life in London and Sporting Chronicle*, 3 October 1863.

9 *Bell's Life in London and Sporting Chronicle*, 1 August 1868.

10 Robin Campbell, *All Bets Are Off: Horse Racing in Swansea* (Llandysul, 2004), 24.

11 *The Cambrian*, 1 April 1887.

12 *The County Gentleman*, 16 April 1887.

13 Mike Huggins, *Horseracing and the British, 1918–1939* (Manchester, 2003), 17.

14 Passage cited in William Linnard, '"Lord" Forrest of St Fagan's: Estate Agent Extraordinary', *Morgannwg*, 33 (1989), 63.

15 *Western Mail*, 19 February 1895.

16 Alan Baker, *The History of Quoits in Wales* (Abertillery, 1949).

17 *Cork Examiner*, 21 April 1924.

18 *Welsh Catholic Herald*, 10 November 1923.

19 *South Wales Daily News*, 25 August 1913.

20 *Western Mail*, 28 October 1899.

21 *Western Mail*, 23 November 1899.

22 *North Wales Chronicle*, 26 November 1859.

23 *North Wales Chronicle*, 31 December 1859.

24 See the letter in *Denbighshire Advertiser*, 18 February 1860.

25 *Wrexham Advertiser*, 11 November 1899.

26 *North Wales Chronicle*, 30 October 1875.

27 *North Wales Chronicle*, 3 June 1876, 24 March 1877; *Western Mail*, 7 March, 19 March 1877.

28 *Western Mail*, 11 April 1893.

Chapter V: Stadiums

1 *Western Mail*, 29 March 1880. This passage draws on research notes written by Dr Andrew Hignell and held at Cardiff Central Library.

2 *Glamorgan Free Press*, 8 March 1891.

3 *Glamorgan Free Press*, 5 April 1902.

4 *Glamorgan Free Press*, 10 October 1903.

5 Jonathan Smith, 'An Introduction to the Archaeology and Conservation of Football Stadia', *Industrial Archaeology Review*, 23 (2000), 55–66.

6 *Wrexham Advertiser*, 10 March 1877.

7 Simon Inglis, *Engineering Archie* (London, 2005).

8 *Western Mail*, 29 August 1889; Williams, *1905*, 60–63.

9 *Western Mail*, 21 July 1891.

10 Clem Lewis, *Welsh Outlook*, 18 (April 1931), 108.

11 *Manchester Guardian*, 21 September 1927.

12 *Western Mail*, 5 April, 26 May 1928.

13 Arms Park (Cardiff) Greyhound Racing Company Limited, *Ledger Book, 1927–1931*, 130; *Glamorgan County Times*, 6 August 1927; *Pontypridd Observer*, 13 August 1927.

14 *Cardiff and Suburban News*, 29 September 1951.

15 Andrew Hignell, *The Cricket Grounds of Glamorgan* (Haughton Mill, 1985), 38.

Chapter VI: The Nation as Playground

1 Simon Schama, *Landscape and Memory* (London, 1995), 469.

2 Alwyn D. Rees, *Life in a Welsh Countryside: A Social Study of Llanfihangel yng Ngwynfa* (Cardiff, [1950] 1996), 140.

3 Today, Wales has three national parks – Snowdonia (1951), the Pembrokeshire Coast (1952) and the Brecon Beacons (1957) – together

with five AONB in the Wye Valley, Llyn Peninsula, Anglesey Coast and Clwydian Range as well as the Gower. Taken together, the national parks account for twenty per cent of the total land area of Wales. This is relatively greater than in any other nation in the United Kingdom.

4   Glanffrwd, *Llanwynno*.
5   Cliff Prothero, *Recount* (Ormskirk, 1982), 1.
6   Trerobart School, *Log Book, 1886–1929*, 14 March 1887, 12 March 1888, 11 March 1889, 2 September 1898, 6 January, 10 March 1890, 11 March 1904; Ynysybwl British School, *Log Book, 1900–1929*, 3 May 1900, 11 March 1901, 12 March 1906, 9 March 1908, and 12 March 1911.
7   Joseph Keating, *My Struggle for Life* (Dublin, [1916] 2005), 1.
8   As above, 33.
9   Edith S. Davies, *The Innocent Years* (Creigiau, 1995), 19.
10 Peter H. Hansen, 'Albert Smith, the Alpine Club and the Invention of Mountaineering in Mid-Victorian Britain', *Journal of British Studies*, 34 (1995), 300–324; Chris Williams '"That Boundless Ocean of Mountains": British Alpinists and the Appeal of the Canadian Rockies, 1885–1920', *International Journal of the History of Sport*, 22 (2005), 70–87.
11 R. G. Sandeman, *Wales*, 30 (November 1948), 624–627.
12 Charles Evans, 'Mountaineering', in Edmund Vale (ed.), *Snowdonia: National Park Guide* (London, 1958), 28.
13 R. E. Griffith, *Urdd Gobaith Cymru, 1922–1945* (Aberystwyth, 1972), 322.
14 R. Merfyn Jones, 'The Mountaineering of Wales, 1880–1925', *Welsh History Review*, 19 (1998), 46.
15 *The Dart: Birmingham Pictorial*, 6 January 1893.
16 *North Wales Chronicle*, 22 December 1894.
17 *Wrexham Advertiser*, 11 April 1896.
18 *Leicester Chronicle*, 24 April 1897.
19 E. S. Chantrell, 'Helyg', *Climbers' Club Journal*, 62 (1934), 33.
20 Oliver Coburn, *Youth Hostel Story* (London, 1950), 29.
21 Youth Hostels Association, *West Midlands and Mid-Wales* (Birmingham, 1963), 34.
22 Taylor, *A Claim on the Countryside*, p. 252. These figures are taken from the YHA website: http://www.yha.org.uk/about-yha/corporate-information/history_of_the_yha.aspx
23 Richard Holt, *Sport and the British* (Oxford, 1990), 195.
24 Hoggart, *The Uses of Literacy*, 298.
25 Steven Thompson, 'The Cycling Craze of the 1890s in Wales', *Transactions of the Honourable Society of Cymmrodorion*, 14 (2007), 114–126.
26 *Cycling*, 1 April 1899.
27 *Cambrian*, 2 May 1879; *Cycling*, 24 January 1891.
28 *Cycling*, 10 March 1894.
29 *Cycling*, 30 May 1891; 8 December 1894.
30 *Western Mail*, 24 February 1892.
31 Williams, *1905 and all that*, 124.
32 *Cycling*, 23 April 1892.
33 David Rubinstein, 'Cycling in the 1890s', *Victorian Studies*, 21 (1977), 48.
34 William Oakley, *Winged Wheel: The History of the First Hundred Years of the Cyclists' Touring Club* (Godalming, 1977), 6.
35 *Cyclists' Touring Club: Handbook & Guide, 1939* (London, 1939), 87–8.
36 E. R. Shipton (ed.), *British and Irish Handbook & Guide, 1892–93* (London, 1892), 73–5; Harvey Taylor, *A Claim on the Countryside: A History of the British Outdoor Movement* (Edinburgh, 1997), 156.

37 Reginald Wellbye (ed.), *Cyclists' Touring Club, British Road Book: Volume 4 – West Midlands and Wales* (London, 1931), 236.
38 As above, 274.
39 H. V. Morton, *In Search of Wales* (London, 1932)
40 As above, 131.
41 Eiluned Lewis & Peter Lewis, *The Land of Wales* (London, 1937), 1–2.
42 *Cycling*, 22 July 1893.
43 Williams, *1905 and all that*, 124.
44 *Western Mail*, 19 July 1892.
45 *Western Mail*, 26 May 1885
46 *Cambrian*, 7 September 1888
47 *Western Mail*, 5 June 1897.
48 *Western Mail*, 23 June 1900.
49 *Western Mail*, 13 April 1895.
50 Williams, *1905*, 162.
51 Ron Berry, *History is what You Live* (Llandysul, 1998), 76.
52 Philip Massey, *Portrait of a Mining Town* (London, 1937), 48.
53 Sean O'Connell, *The Car and British Society: Class, Gender and Motoring, 1896–1939* (Manchester, 1998), 165.
54 Colin G. Pooley & Jean Turnbull, 'Coping with Congestion: Responses to Urban Traffic Problems in British Cities, c.1920–1960', *Journal of Historical Geography*, 31 (2005), 79–80.
55 Welsh Reconstruction Advisory Council, *Interim Report* (London, 1943).
56 Reginald Wellbye, 'Preface', in idem (ed.), *Cyclists' Touring Club, British Road Book: Volume 4* , iv.
57 W. H. L. Watson, *Adventures of a Motorcycle Despatch Rider* (London, 1915).
58 *Daily Mail*, 28 August 1926.
59 The wider history of motorcycle clubs in inter-war Britain can be found in Simon Thomas Potter, 'Motorcycle Clubs in Interwar Britain, 1919–1939: Their Social and Cultural Importance', *International Journal of Motorcycle Studies*, 1 (2005). Available online: http://ijms.nova.edu/March2005/IJMS_ArtclPotter0305.html.
60 Alan Rees, *Memoirs of Merthyr Motor Club* (Merthyr, 2009).
61 Scans of these minutes are included in Alan Rees' book on Merthyr Motor Club, 8–11.
62 These figures are taken from Potter, 'Motorcycle Clubs'.
63 South Wales Caving Club, *Newsletter* 53 (1966), 20–22; *The Observer*, 17 July 1966.
64 For example: Henry Murton, *Recollections of Old Dowlais, 1808–1812* (Merthyr Tydfil, 1874); *Cardiff and Merthyr Guardian*, 28 September 1833 describes footraces taking place at Ogmore Down.
65 Facets of the legend are recounted by Glanffrwd in his history of the local area. Glanffrwd, *Llanwynno*, 103–108.

Conclusion

1   Jason Wood et al., 'A Sporting Chance: Extra Time for England's Historic Sporting Venues', *Conservation Bulletin*, 43 (2002), 4.
2   Martin Johnes, 'Sport in the Heritage of Wales'. Available online: http://hanescymreig.wordpress.com/2011/12/22/sport-in-the-heritage-of-wales/.

Guide to Further Reading

Historians and archaeologists have only recently begun to explore the sporting landscape's rich and diverse past. Every one of them owes a great deal to Simon Inglis' trailblazing book, *The Football Grounds of England and Wales,* which was first published in 1983. Capturing the beginnings of the sweeping changes taking place in football stadiums in 1980s Britain, Inglis combined a keen observational eye with clear insights into the history of the clubs, their grounds and the architects who designed them. Subsequent editions, published after the Hillsborough Disaster of 1989 and the Taylor Report that followed, demonstrated the effect on the shape and form of stadiums in the 1990s. The impact of the Taylor Report and modernisation was not limited to soccer: cricket, rugby and other stadium sports responded in kind to the need for all-seater venues, effective crowd control and fire-safety precautions. Andrew Hignell's 1985 pamphlet, *The Cricket Grounds of Glamorgan,* provides a snapshot of how that sport and its grounds had developed since the 1920s. Rugby was served by David Parry-Jones' *Taff's Acre: A History of Cardiff Arms Park* published in 1984.

In more recent years, awareness of the heritage and built environment of sport has grown significantly within the heritage sector. A pilot project undertaken in Manchester for English Heritage resulted in the first major study of the architectural legacy of sport in a particular community. *Played in Manchester: The Architectural Heritage of a City at Play,* written by Simon Inglis and published in 2004, served as the prototype for the study of sporting heritage in Britain and the present book has drawn inspiration from it. The launch of the *Played in Britain* series shortly afterwards has since resulted in detailed studies of Glasgow (in conjunction with Historic Scotland), Birmingham, Liverpool, Tyne and Wear, and London as well as thematic books on lidos, indoor swimming baths,

C'mon ref! Taken by an unknown photographer at the Arms Park c.1905, this picture captures packed terraces nervously awaiting the referee's decision to award a try or not. Behind the stands are the buildings of Westgate Street including the Grand Theatre, which became the Hippodrome Cinema in 1907.

Britain's Olympic legacy, and the architectural achievements of Archibald Leitch. More information on these and forthcoming projects can be found at **www.playedinbritain.co.uk**. In the case of Ireland, Mike Cronin and Roisin Higgins' *Places We Play: Ireland's Sporting Heritage,* which came out in 2011, provides an important portrait of the Irish legacy including the many sporting remnants of British rule. The project website can be found at **http://irishsportingheritage.com/** All of these books and websites can be read alongside 'Talking Sport or Talking Balls? Realising the Value of Sports Heritage' published in *Industrial Archaeology Review* in 2005 wherein Jason Wood makes clear the value of studying (and protecting) the historic sporting environment.

Aside from the present book, the architectural legacy of sport in Wales is best understood through the many history books, dissertations and articles that have been written and published on the subject in the last generation. For a general overview of sport, Richard Holt, *Sport and the British: A Modern History* (Oxford, 1991) and Martin Johnes' *A History of Sport in Wales* (Cardiff, 2005) are without parallel. Mike Huggins, *The Victorians and Sport* (London, 2004) and Mike Huggins and Jack Williams, *Sport and the English, 1918–1939* (London, 2005) provide detailed and wide-ranging surveys of particular periods and serve as useful comparisons with events in Wales itself. For a detailed work on the role of the Labour movement see: Daryl Leeworthy, 'Workers' Fields: Sport, Landscape and the Labour Movement in South Wales, 1858–1958 (PhD Thesis, Swansea University, 2011).

Each of the major sports has its own high-water mark: Dai Smith and Gareth Williams' seminal *Fields of Praise: The Official History of the Welsh Rugby Union, 1881–1981* published in 1980, which deserves updating to take account of the more recent history of the professional game, is a very important and highly readable centenary history of rugby union. It remains the benchmark for a scholarly yet accessible book on sport. Soccer is best served by Martin Johnes, *Soccer and Society: South Wales, 1900-1939* (Cardiff, 2002). Cricket owes a particular debt to

Andrew Hignell's prolific work in recovering various aspects of its history, in particular his *Cricket in Wales* (Cardiff, 2008) and *A 'Favourit Game': Cricket in South Wales Before 1914* (Cardiff, 1994).

Aside from the big three, the diversity of Welsh sport is gaining greater recognition. Best known is boxing. Well-covered by Gareth Williams and Peter Stead's recent *Wales and Its Boxers: The Fighting Tradition* (Cardiff, 2008), its wider significance can be traced in Dai Smith's continuing work on its cultural history. Essays in his *Aneurin Bevan and the World of South Wales* (Cardiff, 1993) and in his *In the Frame: Memory and Society, 1910–2010* (Cardigan, 2010), illustrate clearly the value of the 'noble art' to the Welsh working class. Andrew Gallimore's biography of Freddie Welsh, *Occupation, Prizefighter: The Freddie Welsh Story* (Bridgend, 2006), with its tantalising conclusions about the Welsh Wizard's influence on the American novelist F. Scott Fitzgerald, is highly entertaining. Speedway is well served by Andrew Weltch, *Speedway in Wales* (Stroud, 2002) and for developments in greyhound racing, Daryl Leeworthy 'A Diversion from the New Leisure: Greyhound Racing, Working-Class Culture, and the Politics of Unemployment in Inter-War South Wales', *Sport in History*, 32 (2012).

Much of what has been written on the sporting history of Wales focuses on the industrialised south. The best insights into the role and legacy of sport in the north can be found in writing on the use of the natural landscape. Merfyn Jones' 'The Mountaineering of Wales, 1880–1925' in *Welsh History Review* (1998) and Alan Hankinson, *The Mountain Men: A History of Early Rock-climbing in North Wales, From its Beginning to 1914* (London, 1977) are amongst the very best. For a sense of soccer in the region see Martin Johnes and Ian Garland, '"The New Craze": Football and Society in North-East Wales, c.1870–90' in *Welsh History Review* (2004).

Finally, there is the wider history of Wales and its historic environment, which provides the context for this book and, through the way it is written, the inspiration for some of its conclusions. The historic environment is best understood through Coflein, the Royal Commission's online database, which can be accessed for free at **www.coflein.gov.uk**, whilst a general guide to its diversity and how it is recorded can be found in *Hidden Histories* (Aberystwyth, 2008). The very best histories of Wales emerged in the 1980s at a time when Welsh history was at its most radical and forthright. Gwyn A. Williams, *When Was Wales?* (London, 1985) and Dai Smith, *Wales! Wales?* (London, 1984) wrote their histories allied to a television programme. Both books and their respective documentary series ruffled feathers and they remain exhilarating reads. Smith's updated version, *Wales: A Question for History* (Bridgend, 1999), brought his version of history to a new audience with little loss of fire. Kenneth O. Morgan, *Rebirth of a Nation: Wales, 1880–1980* (Oxford, 1981) and John Davies, *A History of Wales* (London, 1993), have influenced the present book less but remain key works in the canon of modern Welsh history. Martin Johnes' recent, *Wales Since 1939* (Manchester, 2012) presents a social and cultural portrait of post-war experience. But, in the end, it is in the pages of *Llafur: the Journal of Welsh People's History* that the past, present and future continues to be written and it remains the best guide to further reading there is.

Although it is not traditionally associated with Wales, cricket has long been played in the parks and playing fields of the nation and has a history dating back to the eighteenth century. This Edwardian photograph, taken by Carmarthen photographer J.F. Lloyd, shows a match in progress on the field in Carmarthen Park.

List of Illustrations

Sport is not only about the experience of the spectator and the architecture of stadiums but principally about competition and individual and collective glory. This photograph of a member of Cardiff Swimming Club was taken in the early part of the twentieth century and highlights the wide variety of trophies and medals on offer in those years.

| 35 | DI2011_0413 [left] | 309594 | National Monuments Record of Wales Collection: Wales and Monmouthshire Album. |
| 35 | DI2011_0414 [right] | 309594 | National Monuments Record of Wales Collection: Wales and Monmouthshire Album. |

Chapter 2

36	4954	412833	By permission of Rhondda Cynon Taf Libraries.
38	P002858	33134	By permission of Bridgend Library and Information Service.
39	WPW045173	415374	© Crown Copyright: RCAHMW, Aerofilms Collection.
40	DI2007_1198	34207	© Crown Copyright: RCAHMW.
42	WPW029389	415382	© Crown Copyright: RCAHMW, Aerofilms Collection.
44	3859	414776	By permission of Rhondda Cynon Taf Libraries.
45	23/C/027	415043	By permission of Rhondda Cynon Taf Libraries.
46	WPW029460	306974	© Crown Copyright: RCAHMW, Aerofilms Collection.
47	WPW051608	414696	© Crown Copyright: RCAHMW, Aerofilms Collection.
48	WPW051611	416241	© Crown Copyright: RCAHMW, Aerofilms Collection.
50	PPF15/014	415104	By permission of Rhondda Cynon Taf Libraries.
51	2107	412834	By permission of Rhondda Cynon Taf Libraries.
52	afl03_aerofilms_a7647	415089	© Crown Copyright: RCAHMW, Aerofilms Collection.
54	DI2009_1206	3065	© Crown Copyright: RCAHMW, COI Collection.
55	afl03_aerofilms_a152415	3065	© Crown Copyright: RCAHMW, Aerofilms Collection.
56	DI2010_0041	33112	© Crown Copyright: RCAHMW, COI Collection.
57	23/C/389	415043	By permission of Rhondda Cynon Taf Libraries.
58	P003463	415083	By permission of Bridgend Library and Information Service.
59	P003469	415084	By permission of Bridgend Library and Information Service.

Chapter 3

60	25904	415038	By permission of Rhondda Cynon Taf Libraries.
62	P003457	416189	By permission of Bridgend Library and Information Service.
63	5381	414739	By permission of Rhondda Cynon Taf Libraries.
65	WPW032436	412865	© Crown Copyright: RCAHMW, Aerofilms Collection.
66	31/C/193	33130	By permission of Rhondda Cynon Taf Libraries.
67	25197	413531	By permission of Rhondda Cynon Taf Libraries.
69	449	415818	By permission of Rhondda Cynon Taf Libraries.
70	gb_ivsp_1931_brynmawr_015	411741	By permission of SCI International Archives.
71	gb_ivsp_1931_brynmawr_012	411741	By permission of SCI International Archives.
71	gb_ivsp_1931_brynmawr_014	411741	By permission of SCI International Archives.
71	gb_ivsp_1931_brynmawr_063	411741	By permission of SCI International Archives.
72	gb_ivsp_1932_brynmawr_015	411741	By permission of SCI International Archives.
73	WPW040022	411741	© Crown Copyright: RCAHMW, Aerofilms Collection.
74	gb_ivsp_1938_brynmawr_50	411741	By permission of SCI International Archives.
75	afl03_aerofilms_a206064	412838	© Crown Copyright: RCAHMW, Aerofilms Collection.
77	WPW055458	413329	© Crown Copyright: RCAHMW, Aerofilms Collection.
78	PM1085	N/A	By permission of the Judge's Lodging, Presteigne.
80	AP_2005_1389	33035	© Crown Copyright: RCAHMW.
81	WPW008641	31914	© Crown Copyright: RCAHMW, Aerofilms Collection.
82	AP_2006_039	401391	© Crown Copyright: RCAHMW.

Chapter 4

84	DI2011_0412	21633	National Monuments Record of Wales Collection: RCAHMW.
85	TPS_001	N/A	By permission of Trerobart Primary School.
86	WPW041269	402932	© Crown Copyright: RCAHMW, Aerofilms Collection.
87	WPW029384	412864	© Crown Copyright: RCAHMW, Aerofilms Collection.
88	WPW055396	412880	© Crown Copyright: RCAHMW, Aerofilms Collection.
89	2922	404311	By permission of Rhondda Cynon Taf Libraries.
91	WPW029267	407791	© Crown Copyright: RCAHMW, Aerofilms Collection.

92	WPW008828A	416283	© Crown Copyright: RCAHMW, Aerofilms Collection.
93	Image2-1	23079	By permission of Amgueddfa Cymru – National Museum Wales.
94	1989 8 587 s	33058	Copyright and Collection, Camarthenshire County Museum.
95	WPW040016	415036	© Crown Copyright: RCAHMW, Aerofilms Collection.
96	DSL0002	301661	Postcard produced in 1924, digitised from an original copy in author collection.
97	PM1015	N/A	By permission of the Judge's Lodging, Presteigne.
98	P001191 [above]	415721	By permission of Bridgend Library and Information Service.
98	P001206 [below]	415721	By permission of Bridgend Library and Information Service.
99	GTJ73006	N/A	By permission of Cardiff Library Service.
100	Darylf	3064	By permission of Cardiff Library Service.

Chapter 5

102	WPW038278	3064	© Crown Copyright: RCAHMW, Aerofilms Collection.
104	WPW006052	413426	© Crown Copyright: RCAHMW, Aerofilms Collection.
105	afl03_aerofilms_a78909	412651	© Crown Copyright: RCAHMW, Aerofilms Collection.
106	afl03_aerofilms_a31487	414874	© Crown Copyright: RCAHMW, Aerofilms Collection.
107	afl03_aerofilms_a78933	415115	© Crown Copyright: RCAHMW, Aerofilms Collection.
109	afl03_aerofilms_a78922 [above]	412837	© Crown Copyright: RCAHMW, Aerofilms Collection.
109	N.1990.17	412837	By permission of Pontypridd Museum.
110	scan0010	412837	By permission of Pontypridd Museum.
111	ppf15-017	301664	By permission of Rhondda Cynon Taf Libraries.
112	DI2011_0953	414091	National Monuments Record of Wales Collection: © Crown Copyright: Ministry of Defence.
113	Cardiff Rugby Club 005	3064	Digitised from C. S. Arthur, The Cardiff Rugby Football Club: History and Statitstics, 1876–1906 (1908).
114	DI2011_0968	266095	National Monuments Record of Wales Collection: © Crown Copyright: Ministry of Defence.
115	Cardiff Rugby Club 001	3064	Digitised from C. S. Arthur, The Cardiff Rugby Football Club: History and Statitstics, 1876–1906 (1908).
116	Cardiff Rugby Club 006	3064	Digitised from C. S. Arthur, The Cardiff Rugby Football Club: History and Statitstics, 1876–1906 (1908).
117	WPW029419	3064	© Crown Copyright: RCAHMW, Aerofilms Collection.
118	afl03_aerofilms_a78952	402932	© Crown Copyright: RCAHMW, Aerofilms Collection.
120	afl03_aerofilms_a78439	403220	© Crown Copyright: RCAHMW, Aerofilms Collection.
121	WPW006111	403220	© Crown Copyright: RCAHMW, Aerofilms Collection.
122	scan0006	412837	By permission of Pontypridd Museum.
123	scan0004	412836	By permission of Pontypridd Museum.
124	WPW041267	411733	© Crown Copyright: RCAHMW, Aerofilms Collection.
125	afl03_aerofilms_a165078	411925	© Crown Copyright: RCAHMW, Aerofilms Collection.
126	afl03_aeropictorial_r26110	412895	© Crown Copyright: RCAHMW, Aerofilms Collection.
127	DI2011_0956	411739	National Monuments of Wales Collection: ©Crown: Ministry of Defence.
128	gd0044	N/A	By permission of Rhondda Cynon Taf Libraries.
129	AP2008_3430	402932	© Crown Copyright: RCAHMW.
130	WPW029309	414701	© Crown Copyright: RCAHMW, Aerofilms Collection.
131	AP_2007_1548	309687	© Crown Copyright: RCAHMW.
132	AP2008_3450	309686	© Crown Copyright: RCAHMW.

Chapter 6

134	23-b-018	96245	By permission of Rhondda Cynon Taf Libraries.
136	afl03_aerofilms_a137233	415868	© Crown Copyright: RCAHMW, Aerofilms Collection.
137	DSL0003	408980	Postcard produced c.1920s, digitised from an original copy in author collection.
139	DS2008_179_003	406767	© Crown Copyright: RCAHMW.
140	1989 8 675 s	33058	Copyright and Collection, Camarthenshire County Museum.
141	P001727	301222	By permission of Bridgend Library and Information Service.
142	23-b-006	N/A	By permission of Rhondda Cynon Taff Libraries.
143	PM578	N/A	By permission of Judge's Lodging, Presteigne.
144	DI2009_1278	100284	National Monuments Record of Wales Collection: RCAHMW.
144	DSL0004	301613	Author Photograph.
145	P003275	N/A	By permission of Bridgend Library and Information Service.

146	1989 8 542 s	100101	Copyright and Collection, Camarthenshire County Museum.
147	1989 8 683 s l	100101	Copyright and Collection, Camarthenshire County Museum.
149	N.1990.497	412837	By permission of Pontypridd Museum.
150	5396	N/A	By permission of Rhondda Cynon Taf Libraries.
151	1989 8 546 s	100101	Copyright and Collection, Camarthenshire County Museum.
152	Daryl 006f [top left]	N/A	By permission of Cardiff Library Service.
152	Daryl 004f	N/A	By permission of Cardiff Library Service.
152	Daryl 005f	N/A	By permission of Cardiff Library Service.
152	Daryl 007f	N/A	By permission of Cardiff Library Service.
153	Daryl 010f	N/A	By permission of Cardiff Library Service.
153	Daryl 008f	N/A	By permission of Cardiff Library Service.
153	Daryl 009f [bottom right]	N/A	By permission of Cardiff Library Service.
154	TPS_002	N/A	By permission of Trerobart Primary School.
155	1989 8 594 s	100101	Copyright and Collection, Camarthenshire County Museum.
156	4034	96548	By permission of Cardiff Library Service.

Conclusion

158	TRA0T2	3064	By permission Cardiff Library Service.
160	WPW006115	415072	© Crown Copyright: RCAHMW, Aerofilms Collection.
161	DI2006_1049	3064	© Crown Copyright: RCAHMW.
162	25-aa-017	N/A	By Permission of Rhondda Cynon Taf Libraries.
168	footiebw	3064	Digitised from a print by unknown photographer held in author's collection.
171	img015	N/A	Digitised from a print by unknown photographer held in author's collection.
172	1989 8 648	100101	Copyright and Collection, Carmarthenshire County Museum.

Index

Note: Page numbers in *italic* refer to illustrations and captions.